Scarecrow Studies in Young Adult Literature
Series Editor: Patty Campbell

Scarecrow Studies in Young Adult Literature is intended to continue the body of critical writing established in Twayne's Young Adult Authors Series and to expand it beyond single-author studies to explorations of genres, multicultural writing, and controversial issues in YA reading. Many of the contributing authors of the series are among the leading scholars and critics of adolescent literature, and some are even YA novelists themselves.

The series is shaped by its editor, Patty Campbell, who is a renowned authority in the field, with a twenty-eight-year background as critic, lecturer, librarian, and teacher of young adult literature. In 1989 she was the winner of the American Library Association's Grolier Award for distinguished service to young adults and reading.

1. *What's So Scary about R.L. Stine?*, by Patrick Jones, 1998.
2. *Ann Rinaldi: Historian and Storyteller*, by Jeanne M. McGlinn, 2000.
3. *Norma Fox Mazer: A Writer's World*, by Arthea J. S. Reed, 2000.

Norma Fox Mazer

A Writer's World

Arthea J. S. Reed

*Scarecrow Studies in
Young Adult Literature, No. 3*

The Scarecrow Press, Inc.
Lanham, Maryland, and London
2000

SCARECROW PRESS, INC.

Published in the United States of America
by Scarecrow Press, Inc.
4720 Boston Way, Lanham, Maryland 20706
http://www.scarecrowpress.com

4 Pleydell Gardens, Folkestone
Kent CT20 2DN, England

British Library Cataloguing in Publication Information Available

Library of Congress Cataloging-in-Publication Data

Reed, Arthea J. S.
   Norma Fox Mazer : a writer's world / Arthea J.S. Reed.
     p. cm. — (Scarecrow studies in young adult literature ; no. 3)
   Includes bibliographical references and index.
   ISBN 0-8108-3814-1 (alk. paper)
     1. Mazer, Norma Fox, 1931–   2. Authors, American—20th century—
Biography. 3. Children's stories—Authorship. I. Title. II. Series.
PS3563.A982 Z85 2000
813'.54—dc21
[B]   00-038759

To the memory of my parents
Martha Dishko Staeger
Fred A. Staeger
From a grateful daughter

Contents

Preface

On a cold, sunny March afternoon Norma Fox Mazer and I sat in a hotel room overlooking Central Park and talked about her books, her childhood, her relationship with author and husband Harry Mazer, and her dreams to become an even more gifted writer. We also spoke of frustration, loneliness, fear, and anger. But, most of all, we talked of hope.

Three years earlier Norma and I had met in another hotel room overlooking Gramercy Park, just a few blocks from the small apartment Harry and Norma call home each winter. On that March day, I was preparing to write *Presenting Harry Mazer*. Then we talked of Harry, the books they had authored together, and their many years as husband and wife and as struggling, now accomplished, writers. You can't talk to either Norma or Harry about her or his work without discussing the other. Their lives are intertwined—their work enhanced by each other's input.

At the same time, Norma Fox Mazer is fiercely independent—a feminist. Although she shares all of her work with Harry and much of it with her daughter, the author Anne Mazer, she drafts it first herself. In March 1998, her then most recent book, *When She Was Good*, had gone through many drafts before she showed it to Harry. It had evolved and changed—first as an adult book and then, finally, in the genre she has mastered—young adult literature. *When She Was Good* was her most difficult and painful writing and publishing experience. And, after anger and frustration at Harry's initial response to the manuscript, it again changed from a dark, hopeless book to one filled with pain, but finally ending with hope.

Norma Mazer's books and stories are filled with hope. She is first and foremost an optimist. The mastery she has achieved in her writing is a product of this optimism and hard work. As beginning writers with three young children, a fourth on the way, and no money, both Norma and Harry put in the time to produce endless stories for pulp fiction magazines. These years were their internship—their apprenticeship. It was during these years that Norma Mazer learned how to craft a good story. She also learned how to develop characters in a few short pages so that her readers cared about the people who populated her stories. This was no easy task, but it has helped make her one of the most gifted writers of contemporary young adult fiction.

From her first novel, *I, Trissy*, to her most recent tour de force, *When She Was Good*, readers and scholars can participate in her journey from promise to mastery. In this short book, I discuss her novels, short stories, and books authored with Harry Mazer to show the path she has traveled—a path generations of devoted readers have followed joyously with her. Reading one of Norma Mazer's books is a treat; reading all of them and experiencing her growth as a writer is a privilege.

When Sally Holmes Holtze wrote the first *Presenting Norma Fox Mazer* in 1987, Mazer had written fifteen good to very good books. Holtze felt a need to talk about Mazer in the context of the history of young adult literature, not as a single author able to stand on her own merits. Now, more than a decade later, Mazer has written twenty-two books, several of them outstanding. Today her work can easily stand alone and deserves to be read and studied not as just an example of some of the best of young adult literature, but as the work of an author deserving of our time, attention, and praise.

· · · · ·

The generosity of Norma Fox Mazer has made writing this book fun. The parts of two days spent in New York City with her and the tapes she permitted me to make of our interviews were invaluable— allowing me to include Mazer's voice along with mine.

Mazer also provided me with copies of numerous published and unpublished articles she has written about writing. Her articulate expressions of her experiences as a writer are not only fun to read, but are helpful to writers, teachers, and scholars. She is generous with her time and her talent, and for that I am deeply thankful.

Patty Campbell has been a most patient and thorough editor. She has the ability to make an author's work better without diminishing the author's voice. This is indeed a gift, and I am most appreciative.

As always, thanks to my husband and partner in life and work, Donald Reed. And thanks also to my niece Stephanie who has helped me with many computer woes throughout the writing of this manuscript.

Finally, thanks to Jill Lectka, executive editor at Twayne Publishers, for allowing me to reprint much of the chapter "Harry and Norma: Relationship, Romance, and Writing" from *Presenting Harry Mazer* by Arthea J. S. Reed (1996). [Chapter 4 is excerpted and revised from *Presenting Harry Mazer* by Arthea J. S. Reed, Twayne, Simon & Schuster, 1996. Reprinted by permission of The Gale Group.]

Chronology

1931   Born Diane Norma Fox, May 15, in New York City.

1935   Father blacklisted after strike, family moves to Glens Falls, where maternal grandmother has a bakery.

1946   At 15, meets Harry Mazer, age 21.

1948   Meets Harry Mazer again.

1949   Attends Antioch College.

1950   Marries Harry Mazer. Accepted at Hunter College. Moves to New York City, leaves after six months for Schenectady, New York.

1953   Daughter Anne born.

1954   Son Joseph born.

1957   Moves to Syracuse, New York. Begins three years of night school, University College of Syracuse University.

1958   Daughter Susan born.

1963   Norma and Harry begin writing regularly and publishing pulp fiction for magazines as freelance writers.
Daughter Gina born.

1971   *I, Trissy.*

1973   *A Figure of Speech.*

1974   *A Figure of Speech* nominated for a National Book Award.

1975   *Saturday, the Twelfth of October.* Wins a Lewis Carroll Shelf Award.

1976   *Dear Bill, Remember Me? And Other Stories.* Named an Outstanding Book of the Year by the *New York Times*, a Best Book for Young Adults by the American Library Association (ALA), and a Notable Book by the ALA. Receives the Christopher Award.

1977   *The Solid Gold Kid*, with Harry Mazer. Receives a Lewis Carroll Shelf Award.

1978   *The Solid Gold Kid* named a Children's Choice Book by the Children's Book Council (CBC) and the International Reading Association (IRA) and a Best Book for Young Adults by the ALA.

1979   *Up in Seth's Room* named a Best Book for Young Adults by the ALA and *School Library Journal* Best Book of the Year.

1980   *Mrs. Fish, Ape, and Me, the Dump Queen* named to List of Honor for Austrian Children's Books and receives Germany's Children's Spring Literature Prize.

1981   *Taking Terri Mueller.* Wins Edgar Allan Poe Award for best juvenile mystery of the year.

1982   *When We First Met.* Made into film presented by the Learning Corporation of America and shown on the HBO cable channel.
Summer Girls, Love Boys.

1983   *Someone to Love.*
Up in Seth's Room named a Best of the Best: 1970-1983 by ALA.

1984   *Someone to Love* named a Best Book for Young Adults by the ALA.
"I, Hungry Hannah Cassandra Glen . . ." published in *Sixteen: Short Stories by Outstanding Young Adult Writers*, edited by Donald Gallo.
Downtown.
Supergirl, novel based on the screenplay.

1985   *Downtown* named an Outstanding Book of the Year by the *New York Times* and a Best Book for Young Adults by the ALA.

1986   *Three Sisters.*
A, My Name Is Ami. Named a Children's Choice Book by the CBC and the IRA.
"Tuesday of the Other June" published in *Short Takes: A Short Story Collection for Young Readers*, edited by Elizabeth Segel.
"What Happened in the Cemetery" published in *Visions: Nineteen Short Stories by Outstanding Writers for Young Adults*, edited by Donald Gallo.
"In the Blink of an Eye," published in *When I Was Your Age*, edited by Amy Ehrlich. Receives a California Young Readers Medal for *Taking Terri Mueller* and an Iowa Teen Choice Award for *When We First Met.*

1987   *After the Rain.*
B, My Name Is Bunny.

1988   *Silver* named a Best Book for Young Adults by ALA and receives an Iowa Teen Choice Award.

After the Rain named Newbery Honor Book by the ALA, *School Library Journal* Best Books, a Best Book for Young Adults by ALA, Association of Book Sellers for Children Choices, Canadian Book Council Children's Choice, and *Horn Book* Fan Fare Book.

1989   Edits *Waltzing on Water: Poetry by Women*, with Marjorie Lewis.

Heart Beat, with Harry Mazer. Named CBC-IRA Children's Choice Book, receives The Literature Prize ZDF (Germany).

1990   *C, My Name Is Cal.*

Babyface. Named American Book Sellers Association Pick of the List and Teachers' Choice by IRA.

1991   *D, My Name Is Danita.*

E, My Name Is Emily.

1992   *Bright Days, Stupid Nights*, with Harry Mazer. Named American Book Sellers Association Pick of the List.

1993   *The Solid Gold Kid* and *Silver* listed in ALA "100 Best of the Best: 1968-1993."

1994   *Out of Control.* Named a Best Book for Young Adults by ALA.

1995   *Missing Pieces.* Named American Book Sellers Association Pick of the List.

1997   *When She Was Good.* Named a Best Book for Young Adults by ALA and a *Booklist* Editor's Choice.

Begins teaching in Master of Fine Arts program in writing for children at Vermont College.

1998   *Ape, and Me, the Dump Queen* reissued as *Crazy Fish.*

Chapter 1

The Roots of Realism

Norma Fox Mazer has led a life of stories. As a child of immigrant parents, she learned her family history through tales of hardship and independence told by her Ukrainian/British father and Polish mother. Born in New York City and growing up in a small town in the foothills of the Adirondack Mountains, Mazer's young life was full of people, but often lonely. She thought of herself as the outsider, the observer, always peeking in from around the edges, watching what others were doing. She remembers painfully what it felt like to be an outsider:

> It [adolescence] was a very complex social world with all of the rules unwritten. My understanding of this world was rudimentary, tangled in my own unease, my own sense of always standing on one foot. I was a girl, but not an "in" girl. I had too many strikes against me: I lived on the wrong side of town, I was Jewish. I had opinions. I didn't know how to make small talk or flirt. I didn't have a steady boyfriend. I was "serious," as well, with political ideals. None of these things gave status.[1]

Her parents were Jewish by tradition and atheist by choice. And so Mazer was an outsider in both the large Christian and smaller Jewish communities of Glens Falls, New York. She remembers that her family was not religious and not observant. They did things like eat bacon and shop on Saturdays. The "little world of the Jewish community" disapproved of this.[2] However, both Mazer and her two sisters were bright, and, although they brought honor to the community, they were ostracized because of the family's political beliefs. Mazer suggests that her "otherness" is why she writes—to explore the feeling of being different, to give young readers hope and courage and the knowledge that they are not alone.

Three Sisters

Norma Fox Mazer was born the middle of three sisters. Adele, the oldest, was "beautiful, smart, and admired." Mazer laughs when she remembers that she used to think of ways to kill her off—not murder her, but simply to have her die. Mazer wasn't interested in the gore wreaked by the lumber truck she imagined would hit her sister on its way to a Hudson River paper mill; she was interested in the idea of life without Adele, and, of course, she worked out the funeral in great detail. She smiles as she tells an Ontario audience of teachers, "Well, you know, of course, that one of the pleasures of being a novelist is that you get to work out, safely, your cowardly and mean and terrible thoughts and feelings, your most awful fantasies, your fears, your shames."[3]

Linda, Norma's younger sister, was "a cutie pie with freckles, blonde braids, and a swift, sassy mouth," called Dynamite by their uncle.[4] Norma was in the middle, a tomboy who cried when she was angry, upset, or hurt. And since she often was, she became known as the family crybaby. Although rarely alone as a child, she often felt lonely, cut off from the world of children and adults. There are many cutie pie younger sisters in Mazer's novels, but none of them receive the wrath laid upon the older sisters.

Mazer's novels and short stories, which she calls "domestic situations"—a clear understatement of the depth of her insight—are most often set within families. In her fiction she examines the tensions of her own familial relationships. She talks of seeking a "unity of opposites" within each story. Family members, for example, who should love and support each other find themselves at odds.

Three Sisters (1986), a Mazer novel that has received minimal acclaim and attention, provides an example of an autobiographical unity of opposites. Karen, Tobi, and Liz are sisters who are so close they combine their names to form their own special entity (*Katoli*). Mazer "depicts the intricacies of sibling love and envy and anger and loyalty . . . with depth and insight" in this novel.[5] *Three Sisters* chronicles the complex and intense relationships that begin to crumble as the girls reach their teen years. Norma is clearly none of the sisters, nor are her real-life sisters, Adele and Linda. However, she recognizes that to write a "deeply felt, satisfying book," she must have a point of view on the material.[6] She also knows the danger of writing retrospectively—in putting too much of her own personal point of view into the book—of giving the protagonist the voice of an adult looking back on adolescence, rather than an adolescent looking at life straight on. It may be that the topic of three sisters was too close, too personal to totally remove her adult point of view from the novel.

Mazer fictionally explores other aspects of her childhood and adolescence more appropriate to the genre of young adult literature. In the short story "Why Was Elena Crying?," she chronicles what it feels like to be the crybaby of the family.

Stories of Family

Mazer, as a child, frequently retreated into her world of stories and imagination. She recalls that she didn't differentiate the stories she heard about her family from the real world; they were simply too real—too much a part of her life.

Although her father Michael was reticent, shy, and reserved, traits Mazer may have inherited from him, he told stories of his parents' families. He was born in London, the middle child of three. His parents had emigrated from the Ukraine. Anna Ravinsky and Israel Gamaliel Fox, Norma's grandparents, were married before they left the Ukraine. Mazer is not sure whether their marriage was arranged or was a love match, but she enjoys speculating about it.

Israel worked as a bookbinder in London where he and Anna learned to speak English. Because conscription into the Czar's army was a horrendous fate in which young men often disappeared into Russia never to be seen again, the young couple left everything they knew behind and fled the Czar's agents. Mazer thinks the people of that generation, those who were able to flee, were either "brave or desperate" or both.[7]

One of the ways Mazer learned to tell stories is by asking questions. Even though many questions she asked about her family have gone unanswered, she learned a great deal about her grandparents and their lives through the stories she heard and the answers she imagined as a curious child.

It is interesting to read Mazer's account of the same family story in two different publications. In each the story differs. Why? Is one story true and one fabricated? Of course not. The embellishment a teller gives to a story is the mark of giftedness. Anyone can relate an event; few can make it interesting. She embellishes her stories by changing her responses to questions she asked that were never completely answered. It is easy to imagine young Norma driving her reticent, reserved father crazy asking, "Why, Daddy?" over and over again.

Mazer learned through family stories that her grandmother Anna rarely spoke of her own family in the Ukraine. Michael surmised that his mother had been ashamed of her father who had disappeared when she was a child, leaving her mother alone with two little children to raise. Mazer wonders if, perhaps, her great grandfather was an evil man. Or, perhaps, did the Czar conscript him into the army? She concludes that it is more likely that he ran off with another woman.

Anna, perhaps because of her difficult childhood, was a proud and strong woman. In spite of Anna's commitment to keep a Jewish home, she would not serve a cup of tea to someone she didn't like—an act that most Jews would consider inhospitable, but Michael spoke with pride of his mother's unwillingness to pretend friendship when she sensed scorn and disapproval. Anna was seen by her son as a woman of principle. According to Mazer, Michael inherited these traits from his mother. And, without a doubt, Norma has the same independent spirit and strength as her grandmother and father.

Anna, Israel, and their three children eventually left London. Mazer wonders why. They were doing well; they had made a good life for themselves. Although she does not know for sure, Mazer believes they must have been lonely in London. Everything was strange, and they knew no one. However, they had family in the United States. And so they moved again.

Unfortunately, their lives were never as prosperous in the United States as they had been in London. Israel worked in the garment trade and later had a string of small grocery stores. Finally, he was doing well, but gave up the grocery store to enter a partnership with a man who turned out to be unscrupulous. He lost everything.

Mazer's family was poor, something she did not realize until she went to school. In many of her novels and short stories, she examines what it feels like to be poor and suddenly become aware you are different and are treated unkindly because you do not have as many things as other people.

Jean Gorelick Fox, Norma's mother, was born in a small town in Poland. Her stories, too, are of bravery and desperation. Her mother, Udell Rothenberg Gorelick, and her sister were left motherless as young children. Their father Alexander, Mazer's maternal great grandfather, was slim, and good-looking, and sported a long red beard. When Mazer's grandmother was about seventeen she found a job in a bakery, the first in a long line of bakers on both sides of Mazer's family. She was a lovely girl with sparkling eyes, high cheekbones, and dark hair, all of which Norma inherited from her. She was poor, but bright and energetic. In the bakery she met Aaron, the baker's son. He, too, was handsome, young, and intelligent. His father decided that even though she was poor, Udell was a good match for his son. Aaron, unlike Udell, who was intelligent but unschooled, was desperately in love with books. Rather than watching the bread, he could often be found in a corner reading a book. His father feared Aaron would never be able to make a living for himself, and saw Udell as a practical girl for his impractical son. And so Mazer's grandparents were married. Again, Mazer has many questions about their relationship. The family stories say that Aaron was already in love with the lovely Udell, but no mention is made of Udell's feelings for Aaron. Mazer wonders if she loved him, if they lived happily ever after.

The family stories tell her that their life together was filled with both happiness and tragedy. They had five children—four boys and a girl who would become Norma's mother. For some reason Aaron and his second son came to the United States without Udell and the other children—perhaps to establish a home for them. Udell and the children remained hiding in the basement of a Christian neighbor. These good neighbors, as further protection for the Gorelicks, had nailed a cross to the door of the home from which they had fled as a sign that the Czar's armies had already invaded it.

Mazer has related the story of her grandmother, mother, and three of her uncles in the cellar in Poland numerous times, and the story has changed in the telling. In a speech titled "Growing Up with Stories," delivered in 1984 at the American Library Association Annual Conference in Dallas, she told how the story of her family in the cellar in Poland has helped her understand the Yiddish word *lansman*— literally countryman, but more deeply the sharing of something profound that goes beyond geography. This word, this concept, has helped her understand and express in her writing a belief in the connection of all things—"generations are linked, and . . . life is an endless and ongoing chain."[8] Mazer helped the audience imagine the cellar through words that painted a picture of foreboding. She tells of what the family heard while in the cellar, the noise of the streets, the sounds of shouts and shots. She helps her listeners feel the fear. She relates the unthinkable. Children are by nature curious. It is difficult for them to sit in a cellar and never glance out the window. One day, Max (Mazer is not sure how old he was but she guesses nine or ten) peeks out the window, standing on tiptoes (or, at least, that is what she surmises). A random shot hits the boy in the throat and enters his lung. Although he survives, he is always weak, and eight or nine years later dies of tuberculosis. Mazer has many questions about the incident:

> Did the doctor care for him that day in the cellar? Did the neighbors? Did his blood soak the dirt floor of that cellar? Years later, did the neighbors, stepping into the dark place, always remember what happened to the little Jewish boy?   . . . Did the mother cry over this son, knowing somewhere inside her, with a fatalistic certainty, that though he lived now despite the bullet wound, he, too, would be another child she would outlive?[9]

Although Mazer never knew her Uncle Max, his story has connected her with her ancestors. Certainly she inherited her lively eyes, strength, and dark beauty from Grandmother Gorelick, her love of books from Grandfather Gorelick, her strength and principles from Grandmother Fox and her father, Michael. However, she inherited far more from her ancestors. From their lives, from their stories, she learned how she was connected to them, how she was more than a relative, she was a *lansman*, in the deepest sense of the word. It is hearing these tales and asking questions about them that taught Mazer the importance of stories. Likewise, she learned the art of developing a story as she asked more and more questions.

From these questions and her imaginings, Norma Fox Mazer became the gifted writer of today. It is interesting that she has told the stories of her family in speeches and articles, but has rarely related them in fiction. One published exception to this is the short story "Zelzah: A Tale from Long Ago." This is the story of Zelzah, a young Polish Jewish girl who is sent to America to marry her cousin Jake. Although Jake acquiesces and comes to Zelzah's room at night, he meets an American girl named Grace, falls in love with her, and stops coming to Zelzah. Grace and Jake secretly marry, and Zelzah goes off on her own, eventually to become a schoolteacher who never marries. This is a story from Mazer's family—a story she ends with more questions. "Was she happy? Who could say? Zelzah, herself, never thought in such terms. What was happiness? Did anyone ever know?" (195)

Norma combines many of her family's stories in her first historical fiction novel, which is set in World War II Europe and the United States. It is the story of two young French Jews. Titled *Goodnight, Maman*, it begins in France in 1940 when Papa is arrested simply for being a Jew and Karin, then eleven, her older brother, Marc, and Maman go into hiding. The family flees to southern France on the Italian border when Hitler's army marches into Paris. They run by night through the countryside, sleeping in fields and barns, finally being taken in by a kind, brave man in a section of France that is under Italian control. In 1944 when Italy is defeated by the Allies, Marc and Karin flee across the mountains into Italy, realizing that southern France will now be under the control of Hitler. Maman is too ill, presumably from tuberculosis, and at the last minute does not go with her children. Marc is arrested in May of 1944, but after Normandy he is freed by the Allies. He and Karin are offered the rare opportunity to travel by boat to the United States. Although Karin wants to stay in Europe to find Maman after the war is ended, Marc prevails and they sail to New York on the *Henry Gibbons*. They and several hundred other Europeans are taken to Oswego, New York, where they are housed in a decommissioned military base. Throughout the last half of the novel Karin writes letters to Maman, saving them for her until after the war since she has nowhere to send them. At the end of the novel, Marc tells Karin that he has met a woman who knew the man who hid them. Monsieur Taubert told her that Maman had died of her illness. Karin's final letter to Maman after she has learned of her death is most poignant:

> Dearest Maman,
>   Last night I had a dream of flying. I saw three birds. They flew over my head without any noise. Watching them, I realized I was also a bird, and I became frightened that my wings wouldn't hold me up. I didn't want to stop flying. I tried harder. I watched the other birds. Their wings were beating steadily. But of course . . . I said to myself. But of course . . .
>   Then I woke, and I thought, What a beautiful dream. I want to tell Maman about it. And so now I have. Soon I'll write you again. Goodnight, Maman.[10]

It is a difficult topic and an intriguing story that comes from Mazer's family and her own history through the stories told by her parents, grandparents, aunts, and uncles of their lives in Europe and their new lives as immigrants in the United States.

According to Mazer, "there is more than one reality."[11] Memories are real; dreams are real; fantasies are real; the life of the mind is real. Because of this the stories Mazer tells and writes are more than snapshots, events, or family life. In the stories she heard and the snapshots she saw, there were many realities, all of which find a way into her fiction.

Of Books, Bread, and Back Steps

As a child, the Fox home was full of books, and Mazer read undiscriminately in search of what appealed most to her: a good story. Her love of reading came from her family. Her grandfather Gorelick was a great reader, and in fact, family stories talk about him letting the bread burn in his bakery while he read. Mazer says of him:

> My grandfather was not meant to be a baker. In another life he might have been a researcher, a classics professor, a teacher of languages. He read and spoke German, Yiddish, Polish, Russian, and Hebrew. One of my uncles, the namesake of that red-bearded Alexander, says of him,

"He was a fine man, a proud man, an unusual man. He
was a small man, not strong physically, but every day of
his life he had to do hard physical labor."[12]

She remembers from her childhood that baking bread in those
days was hard, physical work. The dough had to be worked in big
wooden troughs. There were no machines; it was all done by hand. It
was then shaped into loaves, put on long wooden paddles, and slipped
into the oven, which was set high in the wall. It was then that
Grandfather Aaron would lose himself in a book. Her great-
grandfather had been right: Aaron needed a practical girl like Udell.
Mazer's mother worked in the family bakery as a young girl. She got
up at four a.m. every day to wrap the bread and then would fall asleep
in school. When she was sixteen, she left school to go to work.
Although she was not illiterate like her mother, she was uneducated.

However, like her mother, Jean met a bookish man, fell in love,
and married him. A family story about Michael's proposal to Jean
suggests they might have never been married if she had not had to pee.
A week after they met, Michael proposed to Jean. To get away from
him because she had to go to the bathroom and nice girls didn't say
things like that, she said Yes!—although she was engaged to someone
else at the time.

They were married and lived in New York City, where Adele and
Norma were born. They moved to Glens Falls when Michael was fired
from his job as a milk truck driver because he was believed to be one
of the leaders of a strike. Mazer chuckles at that, commenting on her
father's shyness. He never was a leader; he simply was a man of
principle who said what he thought. What he said made sense to the
other men and was influential in the strike vote, so he was
blacklisted—no job was open to him. It was the middle of the
Depression; he had a wife and two young children, so when Jean's
brother Charlie offered him a job driving the bakery truck in Glens
Falls, he took it.

Two of the most vivid memories of Mazer's childhood are the
books in her home and the fresh bread in Uncle Charlie's bakery,
which had been passed on to him by his father. Fresh bread and books
are still two of the major delights of Mazer's life. In fact, she and her
young-adult novelist husband, Harry, still walk most days to a bakery
to get fresh baked bread. And, of course, reading is central to her
existence. In fact, she frequently discusses her need to write—"Maybe
the only thing to be said is that I must write, I need to write, I write to

live, and I live to write."[13] However, she also acknowledges that writing without reading is impossible. "Writing, it seems to me, is always preceded by reading."[14]

Reading was so important to Mazer that she can vividly remember the day she learned how to read: She is four years old and in Sunday School. She is looking at the book *My Big Book of Jewish Bible Stories*.

Some adult is talking; the sun is shining. Norma feels sad about Joseph being so ill-treated by his brothers. He is in a ditch and wrapped in his beautiful coat. She is looking at the picture of Joseph in the ditch asking herself questions about if he's going to get wet. Suddenly, she looks at the "little black squiggles" on the page, and they come into focus. From that moment on, according to Mazer, she was an insatiable reader.[15]

She remembers that both of her parents read every night. Her Uncle Charlie was also a man of thoughts and words. He was always going to change the world. To do this, he kept clippings of many articles in his pockets and would read them to everyone. Whatever topic came up—"nuclear war, acid rain, a new mayor for the home town"—Charlie had an article and an opinion. Frequently his opinions got him in trouble. At fifteen he spoke out in favor of the vote for women. Once he sued the city council of Glens Falls for voting themselves a pay raise. He harassed them for years to replace the Dutch elms that had died with new trees, which they finally did. About twenty years later, Charlie regained the favor of the city council and many of the town's citizens by personally watering each of the young trees during a drought. At age 91, this man who had been considered "an uppity nuisance," called a Socialist—"which he was actually, but it was considered a terrible slander"—and was "pegged as a big-mouthed immigrant kid who didn't know his place," was honored by the city as a "civic activist" and made Grand Marshall of Glens Falls' ses-quicentennial parade.

Mazer remembers many things from those days that show up in her novels and short stories. She remembers always being attracted to people who were different, such as eccentrics. She became acquainted with the homeless people on Broad Street—Crazy Charlie with his bottle-thick glasses, shabby brown coat, and stained baggy pants who spent his time peeling twigs, and Cigarbutt Annie who was short and humpbacked and had enormous thick lips and muttered and talked to herself. She was afraid of Crazy Art because there were stories told about him. She remembers Sylvia, who was brighter than many of the children in school but was crippled with polio. Even in those days, Mazer found it strange that polio-stricken children were separated into special classes.[16]

Almost all of her protagonists are poor, working-class adolescents. The locations of her childhood are also important in her books, frequently adding to the plot and character development. Many of the families in her fiction live in apartments. Most live on streets similar to those on which she grew up—streets on the wrong, industrial side of town, busy streets on which accidents happen and children die. The wooden back steps that led to the Fox's second-floor apartment on First Street are important to both the settings and plot in her short story "Dear Bill, Remember Me?" (1976) and her novel *Up in Seth's Room* (1979).

She not only remembers those steps, but as all good storytellers she remembers events that occurred on or near those steps. She vividly recalls the day the St. Bernard who belonged to their landlord and landlady "took my kitten in his teeth and shook it to death, while I sat on the steps and screamed in misery and helplessness."[17] She also relates that the first time she was commended for her ability to tell stories was one day while she and a girlfriend were playing a game near those steps. Mazer cannot recall the game, but she remembers clearly what her girlfriend said: "Norma Fox! What an imagination!" Mazer says it was at that moment that she realized her imagination had "some other function than to torment me with witches in doorknobs and lurking figures in shadows of the stairs."[18]

The young Norma Fox Mazer was right. The function of her imagination was to tell stories to delight readers of all ages. The places, the stories, the incidents, and the questions of Norma Fox Mazer's young life have made her the woman she is and have given to her readers novels and short stories alive with emotion and humanity. As *New York Times Book Review* critic and young-adult author Barbara Wersba has written, "Mazer is a dazzling writer and brings to her work a literacy that would be admirable in any type of fiction."[19] Story may be the central core of each work, but the living characters make each short story and novel an interconnected work of a master storyteller—a storyteller who can do far more than relate events. Norma Fox Mazer helps us see and feel those events, places, and people so that they become our own, so that they enrich our lives.

Notes

1. Norma Fox Mazer, "Why I Write . . . Why I Write What I Write," *The ALAN Review* (Spring 1987): 50.
2. Mazer, "Why I Write . . . Why I Write What I Write," 50.
3. Norma Fox Mazer, "Why I Write . . . ," *Indirections* (September 3, 1990): 13.
4. Adele Sarkissian, ed. *Something About the Author Autobiography Series,* Vol. 1. (Gale Research Company, 1986): 191.
5. Review of *Three Sisters, Bulletin of the Center for Children's Books* (March 1986): 133.
6. Norma Fox Mazer, "When You Write for Young Adults," *The Writer* (February 1986): 15.
7. Sarkissian, *Something About the Author,* 185.
8. Norma Fox Mazer, "Growing Up with Stories," *Top of the News* (Winter 1985): 157.
9. Mazer, "Growing Up with Stories," 158.
10. Norma Fox Mazer, *Goodnight, Maman,* unpublished manuscript, 167.
11. Mazer, "Growing Up with Stories," 167.
12. Sarkissian, *Something About the Author,* 190.
13. Mazer, "Why I Write . . . ," 6.
14. Mazer, "Why I Write. . . . Why I Write What I Write," 49.
15. Mazer, "Why I Write. . . . Why I Write What I Write," 49-50.
16. Sarkissian, *Something About the Author,* 191-192.
17. Sarkissian, *Something About the Author,* 193.
18. Sarkissian, *Something About the Author,* 193.
19. Barbara Wersba, quoted in *Contemporary Authors.* Vol. 32. James G. Lesniak, ed., (Gale Research Company, 1991): 290.

Chapter 2

Missing Pieces and Outsiders

"To write for an audience, it's not necessary to know their slang or the latest fad. It is important to understand their fears, dreams and hopes."[1] Norma Fox Mazer knows the adolescent audience for whom she writes. For much of her life, she has seen herself as a developing adolescent and uses the events of her own youth in many of her stories. "In the Blink of an Eye,"[2] one of Mazer's short stories, fictionally portrays the events of a day that nearly changed her life—a normal day for a rebellious adolescent. Norma finds a cigarette butt in a gutter and smokes it, knowing that her mother hates smoking. When Adele, her older sister, calls her to dinner, she ignores her. Taking her time to respond to Adele's call, along the way she meets Herbie Sternfeld, the "weird" son of the landlord.

Herbie looks strange because he wears thick glasses and has an "awkward, neck forward walk." His stiff black hair looks like "cartoon hair that somebody shot electricity through." He also acts strange—"he talks in a loud, uninflected voice, and . . . spends his time doing experiments with chemicals in the shed behind the Sternfeld's kitchen." Norma is afraid of him. In addition to all of these "weird" things about Herbie, "he flashes his eyes . . . as if he's sending an important message . . . *A message you better get.*"

This is a typical Mazer description of a character. She attempts to think and write in threes and sees three as a magic number. Threes are very important to her plots, the action rising and falling three times, and the number is also essential to her description of character. She calls this "the rhythm of three."[3] So we know that Herbie is weird in three ways: he looks weird, he acts weird, and he flashes his eyes. We are also told three times that this flashing thing is like he's sending an important message that you'd better get.

Norma and her girlfriend Eva spy on Herbie through the vertical slats of the shed as he mixes chemicals:

> One day, when I put my eye to the crack between the boards and peer into the Sternfeld's shed, Herbie is there again, but not across the room. He is right there, standing by the wall, staring back at me, his face puckered with concentration. He has a hypodermic needle in his hand. Faster than I can take in what's happening, he raises the needle and pushes the plunger. A stream of hot liquid shoots between the slats and into my eye.

Norma does not cry as she runs upstairs to her mother. She does not cry as the doctor says, "a fraction closer, and she would have lost her sight in that eye." From that moment, she writes, "I begin to take the world in through my eyes with a special intensity. It *is* from that moment that I stop crying."

Even in her fiction we learn through her characters of the teenager she was. She has an affinity for outsiders, for observers, for teenagers who have missing pieces in their lives. These outsiders, even though they are different ages and sexes and belong to different families, share a lot of similar traits. All of them, for example, have embarrassed themselves with the opposite sex. Mazer remembers incidents from her own adolescence when she was mortified by boys.

Her characters are also loners—on the fringes of society. If they have friends, they lack a normal family life. If they have a close-knit family, something evil or wrong is hidden from them. They are characters who peek in from the outside. Although being an outsider sometimes caused Norma pain, it also was something she learned to appreciate—it allowed her to use her imagination.

The otherness Mazer shares with her characters allows her to step outside of herself and become one with them. In a new book she is writing, the protagonist will be an older Sarabeth Silver, previously written about in the novel *Silver.* Sarabeth's mother has died and Sarabeth is now on her own. Mazer spoke about the difficulty she has had "getting into" this novel. But, she has no difficulty being inside Sarabeth's head—she knows her so well. She has written many beginnings for the novel, including "Meeting the Mugger," which appears in an anthology edited by Judy Blume.[4] Getting inside characters that share a common otherness with Mazer is easy for her and, for that reason, the characters are real to us.

Mrs. Fish, Ape, and Me, the Dump Queen

Written in 1980, this is a novel about three outsiders. It is one of the few novels Mazer has written in which the adult characters are as well developed as the adolescents.

Joyce, the Dump Queen of the novel, is an orphan who lives with Ape, whom she calls Old Dad. He looks like an ape, hence his nickname, but he has a big heart. Although he has learned the importance of not counting on anyone—of being totally independent and self-sufficient, he has willingly accepted the responsibility of raising Joyce as his own daughter. Joyce, who loves Old Dad very much, is ridiculed by the children in school because she and Old Dad live in and run a dump. Old Dad takes great pride in his work at the dump and keeps it and their small home neat, clean, and orderly. Mazer has fun playing with the setting—a dump that is anything but a dump.

Joyce does not mind the work she does with Old Dad in the dump, nor is she concerned about being an orphan (although she dreams about having a real family). What does concern her is going back to school at the end of the summer.

Even a new girl, Lacey, is friends with Joyce only until the other girls whisper about her. About the same time, Joyce makes another friend, as much of an outcast as she. Mrs. Fish is the overweight custodian of the school who keeps her cat and a tea kettle in the janitor's closet, making it a home. Mrs. Fish quickly recognizes Joyce as an outcast. She gives her tea to sip and takes her into her arms and holds her close. Joyce is comforted; she has made a real friend.

Joyce begins to have lunch each day with Mrs. Fish because the kids taunt her so much she is afraid to go into the lunchroom. Joyce loves Mrs. Fish's closet. She feels just as safe there as she does in her home at the dump. By the end of the book, the two eccentrics—Old Dad and Mrs. Fish—are together, and Joyce is hoping that the three of them will be a real family.

Like most of Mazer's outsiders, Joyce does what would have seemed impossible before. She sees Lacey in the lunchroom at a table by herself. She walks over to her, sits down as if the seat were reserved for her, and begins to talk with her as if they had eaten lunch together the day before. She is strengthened by her otherness and is able to face the world on her own. What makes this short novel so remarkable is that although each of the major characters are eccentric, we feel their anger, pain, and love. As Mary Lystad points out in *Children's Writers*, "They are not your stereotypical family, but they are a fully functioning one, providing love and comfort to one another."[5]

Silver and "Chocolate Pudding"

With the exception of her clearly autobiographical protagonists, Sarabeth Silver may be more like Norma as an early adolescent than any of her other characters. Both are strong, perceptive, and sensitive beyond their twelve years.

Sarabeth Silver, like Norma at that age, is an observer. Mazer says of her own adolescence:

> I laughed and cried and shivered and trembled through my adolescence: tremendous upheavals of feelings, yet all the time the eyes were there, the observer was there, watching, noting, remembering. Yet growing up I didn't value that observer in myself. I only thought it was another indication of what a weird strange duck I was. It was something else I had to hide.[6]

Even though Mazer thought of herself as a "strange duck," she also recognized her strength. Kids made fun of her—even called her a "dirty Jew." Norma didn't have dates and observed the junior prom on tiptoes looking through a window. Although she was on the outside looking in, Norma remained true to herself. She had opinions and was not afraid to express them. She worked hard in school and was a good student during the years when it wasn't "in" to be a smart girl. At about

Sarabeth's age, Norma discovered her love of writing. She joined the school newspaper staff and wrote a column for the local newspaper. Part of her strength, no doubt, came from a supportive family who cared for each other.

Sarabeth has this same strength. Like Norma, she is poor and really does not recognize the poverty in which she lives until she meets other children who have much more. Sarabeth lives in a trailer park with her single mother and her cat Tobias. She was born when her mother was only seventeen. The two of them have grown up together. Sarabeth's father was killed in an accident when she was a baby. Her mother's family blamed Sarabeth's mom for getting pregnant. Her father's family blamed her mom for getting married too young and having to go to work. So, after her father's death, Sarabeth and Mom were on their own. They became more than mother and daughter, they were friends. Two children living in a trailer together.

Like many of Mazer's novels, the story begins when Sarabeth goes to a new school. She is not happy about going, but the night before when Mom is in bed with the flu, she lectures Sarabeth, "You go in there and act like you've always been there, hon . . . Don't let anyone put you down" (7).

Of course, we know what will happen to Sarabeth when she arrives at school, the same thing that happened to Joyce, the Dump Queen. The first-day-of-school scene occurs in many of Mazer's novels, setting the tone for the protagonist's rejection, fear, and eventual redemption. These scenes create a shared experience between readers and protagonists—every teenager knows what it feels like to sit with anticipation and apprehension in a classroom during roll call on the first day of school.

Like Joyce in *Mrs. Fish*, Sarabeth decides that self-possessed Grant will be her friend. The search for at least one best friend is a very important element in all Mazer's novels about outsiders. Grant is always with her other friends, making it difficult for Sarabeth to make an overture. She begins to fantasize about how wonderful Grant is and to write imaginary conversations in her notebook. Grant is becoming an obsession.

However, all of Mazer's female protagonists persevere. Although Mazer does not preach feminism, her conviction that women must be intelligent, independent, and resilient is clear in each of her novels. Sarabeth learns that Grant has a stepfather and doesn't know where her real father is. Sarabeth can tell Grant hates revealing this in class, but now they have something in common. She responds to the teacher's question in the same way Grant did. At the end of the day, Grant comes up to Sarabeth and introduces herself.

Sarabeth goes home with Grant one day after school and is shocked by the affluent lifestyle he has. As she looks around Grant's home, Sarabeth understands for the first time what her mother has told her about being poor and the necessity of seeking opportunities.

Sarabeth continues to be friends with Grant and her three friends. In spite of feeling uncomfortable around Grant's friend Patty, Sarabeth agrees to go to her pajama party. At the party, she meets Patty's uncle Mr. Dexter. She learns that Patty is an artist when she sees the intricate mural she has painted on her bedroom wall. The perceptive Sarabeth recognizes that although it is beautiful there is something strange about the wall painting. The picture has three layers. The first is of a girl dreamily floating, the second of a girl falling, and the third of a girl running away from something. That night Sarabeth begins to believe there is something wrong in Patty's life. As the novel progresses, we learn with Sarabeth the horror Patty faces each day from the sexual abuse of her uncle. Helping Patty gives Sarabeth the opportunity to show her strength and courage and helps her understand the gift of love her mother has given her.

Patty's three-layer mural is a representation of the levels of this story. The first is the story of Sarabeth, her mother, their poverty, and their mutual love and concern for each other. On a second level, it is a novel about adolescence: friendship, dreaming of romance, and overcoming loneliness. However, what makes it special is the deftness with which Mazer handles the third level of the story: the critical issue of sexual abuse, manipulation, and intimidation. *Silver* is written from a feminist perspective, but it never preaches. Instead, it provides its readers with the courage to do what is right and the will to survive.

"Chocolate Pudding," published in *Dear Bill, Remember Me?* (1976), is a short story that lacks the depth of *Silver*, but nonetheless captures the indomitable spirit of a young woman. Chrissy is basically on her own. Through humor and perseverance she overcomes her poverty and is making a life for herself, her father, and her uncle. Chrissy is not ashamed of the tiny trailer in which they live. She loves Dad and Uncle despite their many faults. And, perhaps more than anything else, she loves chocolate pudding and makes it from scratch the old-fashioned way because they can't afford to buy it in tins.

Most of the time Dad and Uncle treat her well, but when things get tough they desert her and go on a several-day drinking binge—she is never sure when or if they will return. In school, Chrissy finds a fellow chocolate pudding freak—Teddy Finkel. One day, while Dad and Uncle are away on a binge, Teddy says he is coming home with Chrissy. All day she worries that the drunks might have returned—repentant and remorseful. When Teddy and Chrissy arrive at home, she realizes by his questions that he is rich and has never been in a trailer. Teddy loves the simplicity of the place, and he has never had *real* chocolate pudding the way Chrissy makes it. "My mother the tennis player buys chocolate pudding in a tin," he tells her (146). This short story points out in eloquent simplicity that life on the "right side of town" is not always as satisfying as life on the other side of town.

Missing Pieces and "Cutthroat"

Missing Pieces is a novel about Jessie Wells, a young girl who has been told by her mother about her wonderful "prince" of a father, Jimmy. One day when Jessie was just a baby, he told her mother, Maribeth, that he was going "nowhere special" and would be back in a few hours. Jimmy never returned, leaving Maribeth with a house and a baby. Jessie, now a teenager, wants to find that father—the missing pieces of her life.

This, however, was not what Mazer originally thought the novel was about. In fact, Mazer had submitted a very different "completed" manuscript to her editor. That manuscript was a novel about a self-sufficient female household—a mother (Maribeth), a daughter (Jessie), and an elderly aunt (Aunt Zis), and how the aging of the aunt affected the family, particularly Jessie. She'd written a few sentences at the beginning of the novel about the disappearance of Jessie's father, the "disappearing dude," as Jessie called him, to help explain why there were no men in the household. When the manuscript was returned, the editor told Mazer in a three-page note that she had attempted to tell too many stories, and they lacked focus. "And, oh, by the way, I'm really interested in that father."[7]

Perhaps Mazer should have recognized the problems in the original manuscript because she couldn't say, in one simple declarative sentence, what the novel was "about." She calls the single sentence that expresses the premise of the book the spine of the story. Around the story's spine grows its flesh and blood. She's not comfortable with her own work unless it has a spine because without it the story will not live. And, in the best of times, she knows the story's spine can say in a single sentence what the story is about before the book is written.

At first Mazer was angered by the criticism of the editor. Her initial reaction was that she didn't care about Jessie's father. However, the more she thought about it, the more she realized, "Oh . . . actually, I'm kind of interested in the dude, myself."[8] So she began to tell the same story again, but this time focusing on Jessie and her father.

Most of the elements of the original manuscript are still in the novel, but now the novel has life. Jessie's friends are there with their stories, although they are relatively unimportant and have been reintroduced, in a different form, in the short story "Cutthroat." Aunt Zis is aging, and although her lack of short-term memory is still an important element of the story, it is no longer the novel's focus. Instead, Aunt Zis's lack of memory provides an interesting counterpoint to Jessie's search for memory of her father. Maribeth is fat and has a boyfriend. The major difference in the published novel from the earlier "completed" manuscript is in Jessie. Mazer finally agreed with her editor that a girl whose father has left her must first deal with this problem before she can face other concerns. So, although the revision was major, Mazer could now explain the novel in a single sentence: "*A girl whose father left her years ago is tormented by her desire to know why he did it and who he really was*" (14).

Maribeth's life had not been easy before Jessie's father left them. She often told Jessie stories about her life, and Jessie used to love to hear them, but at fourteen, Jessie no longer thinks of Maribeth's life story as a fairy tale. Now there appears to be something left out, and from the first chapter of the novel it is clear that she plans to find the missing elements in her mother's story.

When Jessie is given the assignment to research her family in a social studies and language arts class, the die is cast—she will find out about her father. Jessie begins calling all of the Wellses in the phone book. When she tells her mother, Maribeth says it's ridiculous to call 163 Wellses. Even though Jessie thinks her mother may be right, she continues to be obsessed with finding her father and learning about him.

While all of this is going on, Aunt Zis keeps getting more and more forgetful. One day Jessie receives a phone call that Aunt Zis has been found wandering around the parking lot of a shopping mall—she can't remember how to get to her bus stop. Mazer creates an interesting parallel between Aunt Zis not remembering how to get the bus stop and Jessie trying to find her father—both are lost.

One morning before school, Jessie reaches Dennis Wells on the phone—she has found someone who knows her father Jimmy. However, Dennis, Jimmy's cousin, does not know where he is or what he is doing. It is becoming clear that although Maribeth is trying to be supportive of Jessie's search for her father, she is very afraid that she might find him. She is trying to protect her and fails to understand Jessie's need to know who her father is and why he left.

The argument continues between Jessie and Maribeth, neither seeing the point of view of the other. This is a good example of the technique Mazer calls "unity of opposites." Maribeth and Jessie have been a strong unit; they love each other and care for each other and for Aunt Zis. As two members of a three-member, successfully functioning female family, they embody unity. Within any unit, no matter how closely aligned, problems occur, communication crumbles, and differing opinions threaten the group's cohesiveness. A unity of opposites happens in Mazer's writing when problems between previously united characters escalate and threaten their original strong bond. We can see this happening in the final several chapters of *Missing Pieces*.

But Jessie can't stop searching for the missing pieces of her life. She and her friend Jack take a bus to the little town where her father grew up. There she talks to people who knew him and she learns many things that help explain why he left:

> Once there'd been a prince in a leather jacket . . . and a man who wanted a home, a big house . . . and a man who made my mother cry. But before all that, there'd been someone else, too. A boy living with his parents in a trailer . . . a boy who didn't talk much . . . a boy locked out of his home . . . a boy who had to live with other people. I felt sorry for that boy. (102)

One day her uncle, Dennis Wells, comes to find Jessie at school. He gives her a picture of Jimmy when he was a teenager. In that picture, Jessie sees the boy she has learned about—the boy she felt sorry for. She sees a handsome boy who appears ready to leap off the porch on which he is standing, and more importantly, she realizes that she cannot see his eyes in the photograph. "No matter how I turned the photo, I could never get those eyes to meet mine" (112). This foreshadows what will come.

Another day Maribeth comes home from one of her jobs waiting tables at a diner and tells Jessie that she has seen James Wells. He came to the diner like any other customer. She tells Jessie that she talked to him because she knew Jessie would have wanted her to. Jessie sees in this the respect and concern of her mother. James, according to Maribeth, is now a roving computer troubleshooter and plans to be in town for a month or six weeks, but he said nothing about seeing Jessie.

Jessie calls James, having gotten his phone number from Dennis, but hangs up when she hears his voice. Shortly thereafter she sees him in the supermarket buying ice cream. Again, Jessie does not speak to him. "Maybe I didn't say anything because there were so many things I could have said and I didn't know which to choose" (130). She has one other opportunity to speak to him, but even though she recognizes that he is leaving town, she does not approach him. James sees Jessie, looks her right in the eye, but says nothing to her. She'll never know for sure whether he knew her, but she believes he did.

Jessie matures a great deal in this short novel. She learns that even though her Aunt Zis may lose her keys or not be able to find the bus stop, she can give freely of herself and show her love through her helpfulness and caring. She also comes face to face with her mother's pain. She begins to understand how a mother's love may cause her to do things that may not be in the child's best interest, but are meant to protect. And, finally, she learns that not all questions have answers. "But maybe there are some things you can never understand. Some questions that can never be answered. And some things that will never be" (133). "Although this plot has been done numerous times, [Mazer's] skill at characterization, her intricate weaving of subplots, and her ready understanding of teen dialogue and concerns make this book special," said *School Library Journal*.[9]

In the short story "Cutthroat" we again meet Jessie and her two best friends, Meadow and Diane. Meadow and Jessie have been best friends since elementary school, but when Jessie and Diane become friends Jessie's relationship with Meadow begins to change. Throughout much of the novel Jessie and Meadow are struggling to discover a new, more mature relationship.

Frequently, when Mazer is drafting a novel she writes additional letters, journal entries, or scenes to help her better understand a character or a situation. Sometimes these are intended for the novel and are cut in the editing process. Other times these are included in the final manuscript although they were originally not intended for publication.

Some of these have been turned into short stories or used in other novels. "Cutthroat" is an example of this. In this short piece, readers meet the three girls as they are competing in a racquetball game. The push and pull between Jessie and Meadow is obvious, as is the role of Diane as the "outsider" attempting to be friendly to both girls. We see Jessie as the strong individual at the center of the friendships.

The racquetball court, like most of Mazer's settings, moves the plot and helps us understand the characters. This short story is the only time that Mazer, who did not think of herself as athletic until she took up racquetball later in life, writes about sports. Although it is not one of her best short stories, "Cutthroat" is an interesting glimpse into how the writer works—how much time and effort she puts into the development of characters and plot.

Downtown and *Babyface*

Throughout Norma Fox Mazer's fiction it is clear that things are not always as they seem: families that appear to be perfect are dysfunctional; rich people lead lives of emotional poverty; poor families lead rich, self-sufficient lives; eccentrics are more normal than people in everyday business suits. Two novels in which Mazer explores not only the concept of being an outsider but also the difference between appearance and reality are *Downtown* and *Babyface*.

Downtown has one of the few male protagonists in Mazer's fiction—Pete Greenwood, aka Pax Martin Gandhi Connors. The alias gives astute readers a clue to Pete's background. Pax, of course, is

Latin for peace, Martin is in honor of Martin Luther King, and Gandhi
is one of the gurus of peaceful revolution.

Pete lives with Uncle Gene who is a normal, everyday optometrist.
Although it is an atypical family of two men, they live a rather typical
life. Gene is a great cook and an intellectual who helps guide Pete's
reading (we can see the parallels to Mazer's life here). The two like and
respect each other. Pete tells us that "Gene is probably the most
*un*political person in the world" (16). Conversely, Pete's parents, Laura
and Hal, have left Pete with Gene when their politics forced them into
hiding.

Eight years ago Gene received a phone call one night from a
complete stranger who told him that his sister—actually half-sister—
Laura and her husband Hal were in trouble and needed to drop out of
sight for a while. "Can you take their little boy until things calm
down?" (15). And so Pete, then called Pax, came to live with Uncle
Gene. Gene tells Pete that he soon realized the kind of trouble Laura
and Hal were in when the next day he read about the bombing of
Femmer Lab, the death of two people, and the planting of the bomb by
a couple.

Like Jessie in *Missing Pieces*, Pete wants to learn as much as he
can about his parents. His memories are few:

> *Riding Hal's shoulders through a mass of people . . . up*
> *there above everyone else, clutching his hair, laughing*
> *because I was Prince of the Hill on top of my daddy . . .*
> *and all the banners waving and people singing . . . "We*
> *will not, we will not, we will not be MOVED. Just like a*
> *tre-eee standing by the wa-aa-ter, we will not be moved.*
> *. . . ." Marching next to my mother in front of the White*
> *House with a sign as big as me hung across my chest. . .*
> MR. PRESIDENT, I AM 5 YEARS OLD AND I WANT
> TO LIVE, NO MORE NUCLEAR WEAPONS. (19, 20)

When Pete is thirteen he begins reading as many articles about his
parents as he can find. He is not sure what he really remembers and
what he has read about. Pete also recalls some scary moments being
with his parents at demonstrations: "Hal being torn off a pole by police
. . . and mounted policemen riding toward us, the horses' legs as tall as
the sky . . . and running with Laura, who held my hand so hard I
thought our hands would melt together, one hand forever" (19-20).

Gene and Pete keep his past a secret, and Pete has some secrets from Gene. He thinks he's being watched and he writes the sightings in a notebook. Although Pete, unlike many of Mazer's outsiders, has many friends, he is removed from them because of the secrets he keeps.

In this novel, as in other novels by Mazer, there is a unity of opposites. In fact, there are several: the secret Pete and Gene share creates a unity that is threatened by the secrets they keep from each other. Pete's real identity is a secret from all his friends. When Pete meets Cary and decides she is someone with whom he wants to share his life, he doesn't know if he should continue living a lie or tell her the truth and risk losing her.

Mazer uses another technique that helps develop the various threads of the complex plot while maintaining the tight weave of the novel. Many chapters are introduced by articles that Pete has saved in a manila envelope he hides in his room; others are introduced by letters Laura has sent him.

This story is also a romance. One of the many strengths of Mazer's work is how difficult her novels are to classify by genre. *Downtown*, for example, is a problem novel, a story of mystery and suspense, a coming-of-age novel, and a romance. Pete is attracted to a girl he first sees sitting behind the counter at the Nut Shoppe. He learns her name, Cary Longstreet, from her notebook, but forgets to memorize her phone number. At first he tells her his friend Drew wants to meet her, but finally he admits the truth: he wants to get to know her. She smiles at him.

The romance is complicated by Pete's secret and his fears. He is increasingly plagued by the panic attacks he calls the White Terror. He becomes obsessed with finding out about his parents, but he is also growing fearful that he is being followed and that his phone conversations are being recorded.

Finally, birthday letters come from each of Pete's parents. Every year Pete burns the envelopes, and the year he turned twelve he also burned the unread letters. This year he reads them. Hal tells Pete that he is now a man, and Laura sends him a poem from *The Prophet* by the Syrian poet Kahil Gibran. The poem tells Pete, "Your children are not your children" (79). He gets the point, but he doesn't feel like a man. He feels like a child alone, "shivering and close to tears" (80).

One Sunday Cary agrees to go on a bike ride with him, but not before he gets the approval of her very conservative parents. On the trip he begins to understand why Cary seems different: the Yanceys are Cary's foster parents. Cary tells Pete about her family and what it was like to be given up by her mother and moved from one foster home to the next since she was four. This makes Pete feel guilty that he's lied, saying that his parents are dead. The more time Pete spends with Cary, the more he cares about her, but his secret is getting in the way of their relationship.

Pete's fears are legitimate—he *is* being watched. Two agents accost him. Frank Minor, one of the agents, seems friendly and talks about his son, making Pete realize how easy it would be to tell his story to these men. They walk with Pete to a diner, but he is able to break away from them and runs without stopping to school. That afternoon he sees their car again, ducks into a store, and takes a different route home. He begins seeing imaginary agents on every corner.

Pete blurts out what happened to Gene. He realizes Gene is upset when he pulls down the shades and begins rambling on about the past:

> "When you first came to me, every time a stranger walked into the office, I thought, Uh huh! Here we go. I knew just what I was going to say to them. 'Look, I don't know anything about my sister's politics. That's not my thing in life.' I had an entire speech. I used to practice—gestures everything. But no one bothered us. And a year passed and another year, and I thought, Okay, that's it. Right. They're not coming." He frowned. "Pete, are you sure they were who they said they were?" (131-132)

The next morning Pete shows Gene his notebook with all the sightings—a record of license plate numbers. Gene is upset, not because Pete has been hiding this from him, but because Pete has been afraid alone.

Recognizing that his secrets and fears are tearing them apart, Pete finally tells Cary about Laura and Hal: their concern about the earth, the marches they used to attend, demonstrations in front of the White House and Pentagon. He tells her about how they walked out of their college graduation because some general came to speak. He tells her about their raising a flag on the Statue of Liberty just to get people's attention. He talks of their frustration in their inability to get people to listen. Nothing was changing; they felt they were on the edge. He hears himself saying his parents words—words he thought he had forgotten.

"They had to do something that would arouse people, something more than symbolically spilling blood" (142).

At first Cary is upset by his revelation and walks away from him, but later she calls and tells him the secrets she has hidden about her mother. She did have to give her up because she was sick, but her sickness was drug addiction. Both young people have experiences that make them older than their years.

Like most of Mazer's novels, *Downtown* deals with an important issue: what happens when people's ideals cause them to cross the line from nonviolence to violence? Gene must deal with this issue, and so must Pete—each in his own way.

Everything changes when Pete hears on the evening news that Laura has turned herself in. She tells the reporters:

> "I have returned to face the charges against me. Long ago, I dedicated my life to working for a peaceful, non-violent world. Yet, through my actions, two people died. With the passing of time, it has become harder, not easier, for me to live this with knowledge. I don't think justice can ever truly be served in this situation, nothing will bring them back, but nevertheless I feel compelled to pay whatever the penalty will be." (182)

Pete's emotions go from hating her for not letting him know she is turning herself in, to hating her for what she had done, to considering moving to where she is imprisoned so he can be near her. At this point in the novel, Mazer moves the plot along with letters written by Laura to Pete and to Gene. In her letters to Pete, she attempts to explain their motives for the bombing and her reasons for deciding to turn herself in. She also explains why Hal has not made the same decision. She begs Pete to write to her and asks him to come see her.

We are also privy to the unmailed letters Pete writes to Laura. In them he exhibits his anger and his indecision. Mazer frequently uses the unsent letter to help us understand the innermost motivation and feeling of a character.

Pete/Pax goes to New York City to be near Laura. Gene drives him there to help make the decision and the move easier. However, even as they enter the city Pete is still unsure:

"New York City ahead," Gene says, throwing money
into the toll basket.

I look out the window. Soon I'll see her. It's true. I'll
see my mother. A great wave of happiness blows over me.

"Gene!" I turn to him to tell him, to share the moment.
He look at me and smiles. And then I want to cry, I want to
say, Don't take me there, Gene. Take me home!

Home? Where's that? Home to my mother? Home to
Gene? At that moment, I finally understand that there is no
ending for my story . . . no perfect ending . . . no little-Pax-
happy-at-last ending. (207)

"*Downtown* is one of those rare books which explores an
emotionally charged subject without becoming an essay in disguise,"
said Mary M. Burns in *Horn Book* magazine.[10]

Although *Babyface* is not as complex a novel as *Downtown,* there
are numerous parallels between the two books. Toni Chessmore, the
female protagonist of *Babyface,* believes she has the perfect life:
parents who never fight and who love her, and a forever best friend. An
article that appears opposite the first page of the novel gives us a clue
that, as in *Downtown,* things may not be as they seem. The article is
about Toni and her best friend, Julie Jensen. The reporter concludes the
article: "This reporter couldn't help feeling that in these girls and their
friendship and their families, the best of old-fashioned American
traditions persist." The first line, however, tells us because of Mazer's
choice of verb tense that "old-fashioned" values may not be what they
seem: "Toni had always thought of herself as lucky" (1). Mazer has
begun the careful crafting of a tight story.

However, there are also differences between the two novels.
Babyface has a female protagonist who is younger than the male
protagonist of *Downtown.* It is clearly written for a younger audience.
There are fewer subplots, fewer characters, and no romantic interest,
although there is a crush that provides an interesting twist to the
subplot about best friends. Toni, called Babyface by her father, does
not know her parents' secret until well into the novel. Therefore, Mazer
has given the book an omniscient narrator, whereas Pete is the first-
person narrator in *Downtown,* since he is the only one who knows his
entire secret.

One of Mazer's many strengths is the shifting point of view in
which she writes from novel to novel. Many authors write only in one

person; Mazer writes comfortably in three. At times, Mazer even uses more than one point of view in a single novel. (The best example of this, *Out of Control*, is discussed in chapter six.) She frequently changes the person in which she is writing between drafts: first person in the first draft, omniscient in the second, third in the third draft, and, perhaps, back to first in the final draft. Her ability to do this gives richness to her characters and plots. She can get inside each character's head, which then allows her readers to also know her characters. Because she can examine events from differing points of view, the issues examined in her novels are not seen from a single perspective. This is particularly evident in her more complex novels such as *Downtown* and *Silver*. Consequently, the novels never preach. Instead, they provide a broad perspective with numerous points of view.

There are also many similarities between *Downtown* and *Babyface*. Both novels have the same premise: how secrets destroy individuals and relationships. Best friends are important in both novels, and relationships other than those central to the plot add interest to both stories. In each novel the protagonist grows up. And Mazer uses the technique of letter writing in both novels to provide readers with information not accessible from dialogue. In *Babyface,* the letters are used to express Toni's feelings as she writes to Julie, her best friend, who has been forced to move to California when her parents split up. Toni has an interesting and difficult relationship with her significantly older sister, Martine. Martine is the first to tell Toni of her parents' secret. Toni at first does not believe her and later resents her revelation:

> "When I was fourteen, they broke up," Martine said.
> "They'd had another big quarrel and Dad slugged Mom. It was the straw that broke the camel's back." (78)

From that moment on, Toni's relationship with her parents changes. The perfect family she thought she'd had was a lie and she begins to see negative traits in her parents that she never saw before.

> . . . Toni's vision shifted, and she saw, not her familiar parents but two enormous puppets. Puffed-up faces, large, boxy bodies, mouths slashed red, hands like mitts, voices creaking out from behind the masks of their faces. "HAVE YOU DONE YOUR HOMEWORK YET, SWEET-

HEART?" the giant puppet mother said. "WHERE ARE
YOU GOING, BABYFACE?" the giant puppet father said.
Panicked, Toni ran. (125)

Both of her parents recognize the changes in Toni and in their
relationship with her and are unsure why they have occurred. One day,
Toni unexpectedly confronts her parents with the story she learned
from Martine. Both are angry with Martine for telling Toni. "Who told
you?" her mother asked again. "Who told you all this stuff? Martine?
She shouldn't have done that!" (128). Toni keeps asking her father why
he hit Mom. He says nothing. She turns to her mother, asking why they
hadn't told her:

> "You kept me ignorant. I had a whole different idea of
> our family, of him. . . ."
> "Of course I didn't tell you! Why would I? It wasn't a
> happy time. What matters is that you were born, and I
> loved you, we both loved you. We made up our
> differences, we put aside our differences for you." (129)

Toni feels sick, thinking of herself as glue that held their marriage
together—seeing her parents' lives as "pretense and sacrifice" (130).
Finally her father speaks:

> "Why are you doing this to me, Toni?" he said. "You
> think I'm the only man in the world who ever lost it and hit
> someone?"
> "It wasn't *someone*. It was Mom. It was my mother."
> "And I'm your father," he said, his hand still over his
> eyes. "I put you on this earth, and I'm going to tell you
> something, and I want you to listen. I'm telling you that it
> was something awful in my life. You weren't involved. It's
> not your business. So do you think you can forget this? It
> happened once, only once. Once," he repeated. "And
> there's such a thing as being human. Making mistakes."
> Words. Words. Words. She lost the meaning of them.
> She heard them as sounds in her head. Words. Just words.
> "It shouldn't have happened," he said. "You think I
> don't know that? You think I wasn't sorry?" (131)

Mazer creates an interesting parallel between the challenged relationship between Toni and her parents and the changing friendship between Toni and her best friend, Julie. Julie has returned home from California, but nothing is the same between them. Before she left for the West Coast, Julie told Toni about her crush on L.R. While Julie is gone Toni attempts to meet L.R. with the initial thought that she is doing it for Julie. However, she and L.R. become friends and begin to go out together. She has told Julie in her letters she met L.R. in the drugstore where he was working, but she hasn't told her about their friendship or about their date. Finally, she confesses all of this to Julie, telling her she and L.R. are only friends:

> "What's going on, Toni? I couldn't wait to get back home.
> That's all I thought about for months, being in my own
> house again, being with you, everything the way it was
> before. And now I'm here and nothing's the same." (139)

Toni is slowly beginning to realize that things do not stay the same—relationships change. Some flourish and grow; others end. Toni is growing up. However, the resolution of the problems is a bit too quick—too easy. Within the last ten pages of the 165-page novel, Toni makes the decision to work on improving her relationships with Julie and with her parents. She invites both Julie and L.R. to dinner. When Toni leaves the room to give Julie and L.R. time to get to know each other, it is clear that they do not hit it off in the way she and L.R. do. When she comes back into the room with the pizza, Julie announces as if "Toni had been away on a world tour . . . , 'Back at last. It's about time'" (158). It is clear from this pronouncement that Julie sees their relationship as back on track, and Toni is free to purse her friendship with L.R. Although her relationship with her parents does not mend so neatly, it is well on its way to recovery by the end of the novel.

Critic Zena Sutherland writes of the novel, "Although the story has a faint aura of being nicely boxed and tied with a bow, it is believable, it has good narrative pace and flow, and it is both dignified and candid in depicting the discussions between Toni and the members of her family as they work toward improving their relationships."[11]

Outsiders in Short Stories

Mazer is a master of the short story format. She learned how to write short fiction in the ten years she and Harry each wrote one short story or article for a magazine each week. She has written two complete books of short stories for young adults: *Dear Bill, Remember Me?* (1976) and *Summer Girls, Love Boys* (1982). Each of these collections were written as a book—with each short story coming very quickly to Mazer. She says that she wrote two or three additional short stories for each of the books, but selected the best ones for publication.

Both of her short story anthologies have received significant critical acclaim; unfortunately today they are out of print. Pamela D. Pollack says of *Dear Bill, Remember Me?*:

> Death, alcoholism, divorce are unremarkable facts of life in these stories which defy the self-help problem-solution mold and, though boy-girl interest is always there, are anything but romantic confessionals. Quiet and unaffected, these are fiercely felt renderings of misplaced love and search for selfhood.[12]

Other reviews call the stories in *Dear Bill, Remember Me?* "sympathetic views of ordinary, contemporary girls and their relationships with mothers and new boyfriends"[13] and "thought-provoking . . . with a theme of timely and universal insight."[14] *Summer Girls, Love Boys* received similarly enthusiastic reviews. Stephanie Zvirin called the stories a "satisfying collection of nine short stories sandwiched together between two poems reflecting on parent/teen relationships . . . The stories mix the bitter and the sweet of life while encompassing a variety of narrative techniques, settings, themes, and tones."[15] C. Nordhielm Wooldridge suggests that the stories "catch women of all ages at various junctures in life and give equal time to puppy love, marriage and death because all carry equal significance at the moment they occur. If there is an overall message here it is that Mazer can really write a short story."[16]

In addition to her two short story collections, Mazer has written numerous other short stories for adolescents that have appeared in edited anthologies. The variety Mazer achieves in these short works of fiction is remarkable. In addition to those mentioned earlier, this section of the chapter focuses on three short stories with characters who are outsiders. Chapter three will examine several romantic short stories.

"Peter in the Park" (*Dear Bill, Remember Me?*), told by an omniscient narrator, is a story about Zoe. Zoe is not a pretty girl and, although she is well loved, she is lonely—an outsider looking in on life. She has been told by the older women in her all-female household not to go to Walton Park without Marcia (her grandmother), or Mama, or Weezy (her aunt). Zoe, the much loved child in this unusual but functioning family, is about to turn fourteen and is ready to leave, without straying too far, her over-protective nest. Walton Park is a symbol of her family's suffocating love; walking through Walton Park will help her begin to live life.

One clear afternoon in June, Zoe walks through the park and nothing happens except that she meets a young man with a red beard, a little gold cross on a chain, and baggy khaki pants held up by a piece of twine. She learns his name is Peter and he camps at night in the little green station wagon he calls the "Fallen Arch." No, nothing happens in the park that day, and that's what is important to Zoe. Zoe does not tell Mama, or Marcia, or Weezy about her walk in the park or about the man who calls her Goldie because of her blond braids.

Zoe continues to walk through the park, even planning to risk missing her traditional birthday breakfast to see Peter. But she sleeps late that day, and by the time she pulls on her jeans and gets to the kitchen, Weezy, Mama, and Marcia are at the breakfast table with pancakes and presents. All day long they entertain her—even taking her to a movie and serving her a steak dinner. During the night Zoe wakes up and decides to walk to the park to see Peter. Weezy hears her leaving and tries to stop her, not knowing where she is going. All the way down the dark, rain-soaked streets she imagines Peter's greeting, but when she gets to the park Peter is gone. "She's all alone in the middle of the night in Walton Park" (53). For the first time she is afraid, but nothing happens. When she gets home, every light in the house is blazing, everyone is up waiting for her. They are not angry; they are concerned and want to know where she has been. Zoe does not tell them—she can't tell them. Zoe has begun to live life—to walk in Walton Park.

"Mimi the Fish" (*Dear Bill, Remember Me?*) begins with an entry from the dairy of Mimi Holtzer. She is an outsider who thinks of herself as a fish swimming through a "murky sea." She keeps trying to swim to the light, but she can't make it to the top. Her mother keeps talking to Mimi about when she herself was a teenager—all the dates she had and the parties she gave. She wants Mimi to give a party—she wants to live her life through Mimi. But Mimi can't throw a party. First, she doesn't have anyone to invite, and second, she lives in a house with a butcher shop in the front where most people's living room would be. How can she give a party there?

One night, in spite of looking like a "plain, skinny, drink-of-water," (89) Mimi encounters the unbelievable. The wonderful, beautiful R.R., subject of the notes Mimi and her best friend Susan pass, calls Mimi and asks her to come to a dance at the Y that evening.

She worries that it was not really Robert Rovere on the phone, but when he arrives at her home that night and meets her parents they ask the unthinkable: "We got a case of imported Limburger in today, Robert. Straight from Belgium. We get it only for our special customers. Mimi, I promised Milly you'd deliver it tonight" (94). Although Mimi protests that they are not going that way, Robert says that it is fine, they will take the cheese. Unfortunately, Mimi does not know that Milly has moved, and they go to the wrong house. "She hated to admit it, but the cheese would have to go to the dance with her." (97)

And, so it does, on her first date ever with the handsome R.R. Mimi's date with Robert is reminiscent of one of Norma's first dates. The entire evening they did not speak—not one word. For years, she worried about running into that boy—by then a man—and having him remember who she was—the girl without a voice. Mimi and Robert speak, but because of the limburger cheese she embarrasses herself in front of him:

> Several people glanced strangely at her. She was hot, sweating. The odor rising from her jacket was growing stronger by the moment. She tried planning how she would tell Susan about all this. . . . *It was really funny, I felt like turning into a lump of Limburger myself. Only he didn't think it was funny. What can you expect? No sense of humor. Blah.* . . . (101)

But Robert does have a sense of humor. When kids start saying, "Something *stinks*," Robert replies, "I don't smell anything . . . You, Mimi?" (102). The date is not a disaster at all:

> "I'm sorry about the cheese," she said.
> "Cheese? What cheese?" he said, and he kissed her. (103)

When Mimi arrives home her mother wants to hear all about the dance, the kids who were there, and good-looking Robert. But Mimi says she is tired and does not want to talk about it. When she finally tells her mother about the cheese, her mother is mortified and feels guilty. She cries and holds Mimi in her arms, and Mimi lets her do it; she recognizes that her mother cannot protect her much longer. But she doesn't tell her about the dance, about Robert, or about the kiss:

> She was moving away from her mother, out of this life, these closed rooms, swimming free, swimming toward her own life, into her own blue sea. Swimming strongly and freely away. Mimi the fish! Good-bye, she sang in fish language. Good-bye, good-bye! (107-108)

"I, Hungry Hannah Casssandra Glen . . ." appears in *Sixteen*, an anthology of short stories by writers of young adult fiction, edited by Donald Gallo. This is the story of two outcasts—two outcasts who are hungry. The story is told in first person by Hannah. She convinces her friend Crow, who is not only hungry but has an unidentified problem with his face, to attend the funeral of Mr. Augustus Francher, owner of a local grocery, because "afterward at Mrs. Francher's house, there would be food" (2). Crow attends without enthusiasm.

When they shake hands with Mrs. Francher after the funeral they are not invited to her home, but they hear everyone else in the receiving line being invited. So, while the other people at the funeral service go to the graveyard, Hannah and Crow wait outside Mrs. Francher's home fantasizing about the food that is within. When the cars return from the funeral, Mrs. Francher invites the two of them inside. Once they are inside, Mazer helps us understand why two hungry youngsters would want to be invited to the home after the funeral:

A long table, loaded with food, took up almost the whole dining room. I squeezed Crow's hand. Our quarrel was forgotten. In the center of the table were two crystal bowls, one filled with apples, pears, grapes, and bananas, the other brimming with fizzing red punch. There were platters of roast beef, ham, turkey, and salami, little fluted cups filled with butter, a wooden board with a cutting knife, and different kinds of cheeses. There was applesauce and fruit salad, baked potatoes wrapped in silver paper, tomatoes and cucumbers, bread and rolls and cakes and all kinds of hot casseroles. (13)

The two hungry children eat until they can eat no more and then they fill their pockets with food to take home to their hungry families. On the way out Hannah thinks that she feels no guilt about "how glad I was that Mr. Francher had died and left us this feast" (13). She imagines him looking at her from his coffin and saying to her what he used to say when she came into his grocery store, "Now, daughter, now daughter. . . ." (13)

Notes

1. Norma Fox Mazer, "When You Write for Young Adults," *The Writer* (February 1986): 15.
2. Norma Fox Mazer, "In the Blink of an Eye," in *When I Was Your Age: Original Stories About Growing Up,* Vol. 2. Amy Ehrlich, ed. (Candlewick Press, 1998): 14-31.
3. Norma Fox Mazer, "When You Write for Young Adults," 16.
4. Norma Fox Mazer, "Meeting the Mugger," in *Places I Never Meant to Be*, Judy Blume, ed. (Simon & Schuster, 1999).
5. Mary Lystad, review of *Mrs. Fish, Ape, and Me, the Dump Queen*, *Twentieth-Century Children's Writers* (1989): 652.
6. Norma Fox Mazer, "Letters to Me," *The ALAN Review* (Spring 1990): 8-9.
7. Norma Fox Mazer, "Breathing Life into a Story," *The ALAN Review* (September 1995): 14.
8. Mazer, "Breathing," 14.
9. Cindy Darling Codell, review of *Missing Pieces*, *School Library Journal* (April 1995): 154.

10. Mary M. Burns, review of *Downtown, Horn Book* (January/February 1985): 61.

11. Zena Sutherland, review of *Babyface, Bulletin of the Center for Children's Books* (November 1990): 65.

12. Pamela D. Pollack, review of *Dear Bill, Remember Me? School Library Journal* (October 1976): 191.

13. Review of *Dear Bill, Remember Me?, Kirkus Reviews* (October 1, 1976): 1101-1102.

14. Ann A. Flowers, review of *Dear Bill, Remember Me? Horn Book* (February 1977): 58-59.

15. Stephanie Zvirin, review of *Summer Girls, Love Boys, ALA Booklist* (October 1, 1982): 198-199.

16. C. Nordhielm Wooldridge, review of *Summer Girls, Love Boys, School Library Journal* (November 1982): 102.

Chapter 3

Star-Crossed Love

Norma Fox Mazer's romance novels for young adult readers are anything but typical teenage romances in which girl gets boy, girl loses boy, and girl gets boy—who has changed for the better—back again. Although Mazer's stories have action that rises and falls three times, the events leading to the rising and falling action are not necessarily related to the romance. In each of Mazer's romance novels an important issue is front and center—the "spine" around which the flesh and the blood of the book grows. In addition, Mazer's romances have many subplots: friendships, sibling rivalries, and conflicts with parents. The settings are not typical either. The young characters are from working-class families, and sometimes they, too, are members of the working class. Their homes and apartments are the places of Mazer's youth and young married life. Mazer has written three romance novels on her own and two with her husband, Harry Mazer. (Those books will be discussed in chapter 4.) Many of her other novels have romantic elements; however, in those novels the romance is secondary to the major premise.

Up in Seth's Room

Up in Seth's Room, written in 1979, was Mazer's first effort at novel-length romantic fiction. Before *Dear Bill, Remember Me*, her third book, she was terrified each time she started a new work. Her newfound confidence is evident in *Up in Seth's Room*, the story of a romance between an older boy who is ready for sex and a younger girl who is not. Mazer claims to have written the book as a response to the explicit sexuality of Judy Blume's *Forever*. Although Mazer respected Blume's novel, she also believed there were many teenage girls who were not ready to make the emotional commitment of a consummated relationship. Mazer was convinced that someone needed to write a book for these girls—not a book that ignored the sexual drive of the young, as earlier young adult novels had, but one that spoke of sex in an honest way.

The fact that Mazer raised three daughters may have helped solidify her conviction that this story needed to be told. It was not an easy story to tell in 1979 when critics were praising the sexuality in young-adult coming-of-age novels. Criticism of *Up in Seth's Room* bore this out. Critic and author Jean Fritz wrote in the *New York Times Book Review*, "The questions we follow relentlessly from beginning to end are the perennial ones of adolescence: Will she or won't she? And what's it like? . . . Everyone should be pleased with the outcome. Finn sticks to her guns, although the fact that she 'doesn't' is hardly more than a technicality."[1]

The story begins when fifteen-year-old Finn Rousseau goes to visit her older sister, Maggie, who is living with her boyfriend Jim. There Finn meets Jim's younger brother, Seth.

Mazer's description of Seth, through Finn's eyes, is a good example of her ability to make a character come to life:

> But Seth was lean and dark, and the way he was sitting on the couch, legs crossed, hands resting gracefully on his thighs, he looked more like a prince out of a fairy tale than any dropout Finn knew. Except, of course, for the faded jeans and scuffed work boots. (4)

And Mazer describes him a second time:

> He had a great voice! Deep and warm . . . He was good-looking enough for half a dozen guys. (4)

And, lest we have missed his good looks, she describes him once again:

> Bet anything he knows how good-looking he is, Finn thought. All that dark hair and those cheekbones and full, red lips. She decided she didn't like him. Tooo, to*oo, too* good-looking. (5)

By the end of this first chapter, we have been introduced to Seth, and we learn he will be staying in town looking for a job. We have discovered that Maggie is the beautiful sister. "You two don't look at all alike," Toby said . . . "Maggie's beautiful. . . . You're not jealous?" (6-7). Finn, at fifteen, is tall, five feet nine, with long legs. Her mother calls her "coltish." She has straw-colored hair that she wears in a horsetail. She thinks she looks more like a horse than a colt, she isn't delicate like a colt. "Besides, when she smiled, she felt that she showed a lot of teeth" (2). We also learn in the first chapter that Finn's parents do not approve of Maggie living with Jim. In fact, they do not speak to her. And by the end of the chapter, we also learn that Finn does not dislike Seth as much as she thought she did. When Finn walks down the steps with Maggie, she learns that Seth is nineteen. She tells Maggie, "He's cute" (11).

One of Finn's friends, Vida, is trying to pair her up with Jerry Demas. At a New Year's Eve party, Finn tells her friends about Seth. "You should see Seth, Vida. He's gorgeous" (15). At the party Finn and Jerry get together. They have a few drinks of spiked punch, they kiss, and Jerry attempts to seduce Finn.

The next day Finn sees Seth again when she goes with Maggie, Jim, and Seth to a New Year Polar Bear Dip. Their relationship is developing. And we learn more about Seth and the tension between him and his family.

Finn tells her friends about Seth and is beginning to fantasize about him. However, when Seth comes by in his green VW bug, he acts like he can't remember Finn's name, and she is humiliated in front of friends. When she confronts him he apologizes and says he is really down because he's been looking for a job and hasn't found one. This incident shows the readers and Finn the difference in their maturity—he has serious things like a job on his mind, and "she'd been acting like a nit" (42). Nonetheless, she begins to obsess about Seth.

In the library, Finn is trying to study but is thinking about Seth when he comes up and touches her on the shoulder, asking her for a date. We now have the first rise in the action—the romance is about to begin.

Finn is afraid to tell her mother about the date, not only because Seth is older, but because he is Jim's brother. Finally she does. Her mother gives Finn the third degree, and when she learns that Seth has dropped out of school and is nineteen she tells her daughter, "No, Finn. Forget it" (62).

The conflict has been introduced—the action falls. Finn has every intention of seeing Seth, but she will have to sneak around to do so. She will have to lie to her parents. The next afternoon she goes to the cafeteria where Seth has found a job to tell him her mother won't let her go. For the first time, Seth learns that Finn is fifteen. She leaves the restaurant in the midst of an argument with him about whether she is too young.

On the Friday night of the supposed-to-be date with Seth, Finn goes to a rock concert with Vida and her boyfriend Paul. They become separated. Seth tugs at her sleeve just as it has been announced that the group has been delayed by a blizzard and the concert is canceled. Seth waits with Finn for her mother to pick her up and he makes it clear that he wants to see her again. Just as she sees her mother's car approach, Seth turns to her and kisses her. This time she is an active, willing participant.

Seth and Finn agree to meet at Maggie's—her parents can't forbid her to see her sister—and at the cafeteria where Seth works. When Finn's mother asks where she has been, Finn lies, telling her she's been with Vida shopping for a blouse.

Most days for the next several weeks Finn sits at a table at the corner of the cafeteria, drinking a hot chocolate and doing her homework until Seth can join her. Then they talk, hold hands, and kiss. Some days she calls Seth on her lunch hour, and some days she leaves school early. They meet on Friday nights at the movies. Finn tells her mother that she is going with Vida and Vida covers for her. Vida tells Finn that she and Paul have had intercourse.

Finn recognizes the irony in what is happening. Her parents would have no objection to her seeing Jerry, and he pushes her to have sex like Paul and Vida. They won't let her see Seth because they are afraid he will "take advantage" of her because he thinks she's like Maggie. Even Maggie expresses her concern about Finn seeing Seth.

She suggests to Finn that at fifteen she is susceptible and can be pushed into doing things.

Then the situation begins to change. Seth and Finn go to the art museum, to a bench in an area where almost no one goes. They kiss. Seth tries to convince Finn to take off her blouse, leaving her coat on, so he can fondle her breasts. They fight. She feels guilty for spoiling his pleasure. They talk about sex—about all the girls he's made love to. And he tells Finn that none of them compare to her.

Seth's boss tells Finn not to come to the cafeteria. Seth quits his job, and they meet in Maggie's apartment. Jim comes home and tells Finn she shouldn't be there. Jim and Seth fight. Seth not only runs away from Jim and the apartment, but from Finn, too. For several days they do not speak or see each other, but then Seth calls and they agree to meet. Seth has a new job and has rented an attic room. At first she doesn't want to lie down next to him on the bed, but he convinces her that if she doesn't want anything to happen it won't. They have sex without having intercourse. Finn tells Seth she likes it.

Things quickly escalate between Seth and Finn now that he has his own room and they have privacy. Even though her parents find out they've been seeing each other and a terrible battle ensues, resulting in Finn's being grounded, she still finds ways to see Seth. In one climatic scene, Seth comes close to raping her. He keeps telling her that her refusal to have intercourse is because she is only thinking about herself.

"You think it's right to shoot off into the wall?" he asks her. This angry comment hurts her more than anything else. The last time they'd been together, he had told her it had been beautiful—now he was saying he'd lied. She breaks away from him and runs out of the apartment.

They don't see each other for some time. When they do, Seth apologizes to her, but it is clear that it is not totally sincere:

> "It's just that—everyone knows you have to convince girls—" His face was reddening. "Okay, I know I didn't act too wonderfully. But under the circumstances . . . that's a very tense situation for a man." (182)

During that same conversation, Seth tells her that he is going to be moving to Vermont to work on a farm. Although the conversation is satisfying for neither of them, they part as friends.

They see each other again at a party. Seth tells Finn he's been doing a lot of thinking about what happened:

> "I'll tell you—I always thought we'd make love— . . . For a long time now any girl I go with, I sleep with."
> "Did they all want to?" she said. She couldn't be the only girl in the world who wanted to wait until she was older.
> "I always thought so," he said. "I don't know, maybe they were just going along. I always figured the thing to do was try, just keep trying. You know. If at first you don't succeed . . . that's the male creed.
> . . . the macho thing to do with a girl is never take no for an answer. Just keep trying. Wear her down one way or the other."
> "That's ugly," she said.
> "I know," he said. . . . . "The only thing I can figure is that somehow I've gotten the idea that sleeping with a girl is the *only* thing that counts." (190)

They decide that they will try to have sex without intercourse. Finn realizes that Seth is not as sure about things as he sounds; he talks about it as an experiment with an unsure outcome. The final action occurs in the last chapter of the book. Seth and Finn drive into the country and walk hand-in-hand into a field. He tells Finn that he is leaving the next day for Vermont. Their good-bye is to have sex together in a way that is good for both of them.

> They took off their clothes. Naked, they knelt together, their knees touching. She put her hands on his shoulders. He held her waist. Then they lay down together. There was the smell of crushed grass and dandelions.
> Fingers . . . hands . . . lips . . .
> "Oh . . . now!" He turned away. He was singing. He always sang. She had her arms around him, her face pressed against his back. She floated in golden circles, spinning higher and higher, the circles narrowing and golden, dazzling. (197)

If there is a message in this novel, this is it: sex without intercourse is possible and may be preferable for the young. Shortly after the novel was published, Mazer wrote about it in an article:

The young are full of passion for a sexual life; but does
that have to mean "doing it"? Don't we use the word *sex*
in too narrow a way? As if sex is simply a quicker way of
saying that cumbersome word *intercourse*? As if sex
equals intercourse? But of course there's a great deal more
to sex than this. This is something young people need to
know.

Intercourse, the ultimate intimacy, catapults two
people into a relationship that demands a high degree of
responsibility and responsiveness. And for adolescents this
comes at the very time when they are most changeable,
volatile, vulnerable; most easily bruised. I'd like to see
kids wait, not for sex, but for intercourse.[2]

Mazer's comments may have been in response to the criticism of
the novel. Patty Campbell calls Finn's and Seth's relationship "a
grotesque battle over whether she is willing to let him—as they say in
the sex manuals—achieve penetration." Campbell compares the
book's "agonies and yearnings of sexual avoidance" to Maureen
Daly's *Seventeenth Summer* written thirty years earlier. She calls
Finn's protection of "her technical virginity" and acceptance of "every
other form of intimacy with cheerful enthusiasm" a medieval attitude.[3]

Another reviewer suggests that *Up in Seth's Room* presents a
"cliché situation, with some goopy descriptions of sexual bliss and
what might well be seen as a ludicrous solution these days when
technical virginity has pretty much lost its cachet."[4]

One of the things the reviewers of *Up in Seth's Room* miss in the
novel is the strength of Finn. She remains true to herself. She has told
Seth from the beginning that she is not ready for intercourse. When
he attempts to "wear her down one way or the other" (190), she resists
as no girls before her had. This has to be very difficult for Finn, who is
in love with Seth—she knows that her unwillingness to "do it" may
end the relationship. However, she remains strong, and like all
Mazer's female protagonists she is older than her years, stronger than
those around her expect her to be. She has a hidden fortitude that she
recognizes, but questions, too.

The reviews of *Up in Seth's Room* were clearly of their time—the
1970s sexual revolution. Even the term "technical virginity" was of the
1970s. Today, however, reviewers might receive this book differently.
In fact, it might be reviewed as a book on date rape. A more favorable
review in *Booklist* made reference to "an encounter that stops just
short of force"[5]—what in the 1990s was called date rape. Finn had

clearly indicated her willingness to be in Seth's room, even on Seth's bed, but she had also made it clear that she was not ready for the ultimate intimacy. Even Seth seems to recognize that the sex he has had with other girls may not have been what they wanted, but the result of the male creed, "if at first you don't succeed . . . " (190), and their unwillingness to fight. *Up in Seth's Room* is a novel that was ahead of its time rather than behind the time.

Someone to Love

Someone to Love (1983) could be Finn's story if she had been four years older. In fact, it is the same story, coming to the same conclusion—intimacy requires more than love and passion, it requires commitment, patience, responsibility, and responsiveness. However, this novel has a totally different premise than the earlier novel: A lonely college freshman meets a lonely university dropout, they are attracted to each other, move in together, and find that living together is not as easy as they thought it would be.

Of Mazer's three romances, *Someone to Love* has the simplest structure, with a minimum of subplots. Its action rises and falls three times, but its denouement is predictable.

As in *Up in Seth's Room*—and as Norma and Harry Mazer were themselves—the lovers are on different levels. Nina Bloom is a serious college student; Mitchell Beers is a college dropout who is making a living as a house painter. Both of them are lonely. Keeping her relationship with Mitch from her parents is easier for Nina than it was for Finn, but no less damaging to their developing romance.

Mitch Beers was borrowed from Mazer's earlier novel, *I, Trissy.* Mazer frequently uses the technique of importing a character from one novel to another. In the earlier novel Mitch played the minor role of Trissy Beers' obnoxious brother. His parents had split up, and we learn in *Someone to Love* that their divorce was as devastating for him as it had been for Trissy. Reviewers frequently praise her characterization. Audrey B. Eaglen calls Nina and Mitch, "believable characters with whom young adult readers will empathize and understand."[6] Mary K. Chelton says that the "characterizations are superb, without a wasted word."[7]

Nina lives away from home in a walk-up apartment with two music majors, Lynell and Sonia. She feels like an outsider in her own apartment. Lynell and Sonia go everywhere together; they share similar interests. Nina's best friend is her cat, Emmett, and she feels left out:

> Of course, Nina told herself, she couldn't expect not to be a *bit* of an outsider. But in truth, it wasn't only with her roommates that she felt this way. She had become acutely aware of how little she knew about a whole range of subjects—and how restricted her life had been. She stayed up studying and woke up early worrying about marks and papers and all the books on her reading lists. She was keeping up, but was never at ease, terrified all the time of failing. To fail would be worse than the failure itself: it would mean going back home with her head hanging, back to Community College of the Mountains, where she'd spent her first year, back to her parents' house, where her father still wore his invalid's slippers and her mother, bitter and proud, kept what remained of their family together. (8)

Nina, like most of Mazer's characters, comes from a poor family, although not "bone poor," she tells us. Since her father's surgery they have lived on her father's disability insurance check. She must work very hard to escape from her family's background, and can't afford the time to attend concerts and parties, the time to make friends. And so Nina is vulnerable. She is seeking a way to enlarge her world and her experiences; she is searching for someone to love.

Mitch, on the other hand, comes from a family of achievers. His father is a professor, so everyone assumed he would go to college. He did; he was majoring in pre-law, but dropped out his junior year. Like Nina and Seth, he is rebelling against the expectations of his family. He tells Nina that there are lots of things other than college, that he loves working with his hands.

Before Nina meets Mitch, we learn of her favorite professor:

> Her first day in his class she'd thought he looked exactly the way a professor should look—worn tweed jacket, salt and pepper beard, and he even had a pipe. His manner, too, was satisfying. As he lectured he roamed the room,

streaking his hands through his hair, pulling at his tie, and
pounding desks to make his point. (14)

Professor Lehman fits Nina's stereotype, and we know he will play a
role in the story.

Nina's and Mitch's first date should be a warning of things to
come. They can't seem to agree on anything to do but when they begin
talking about themselves, their families, and their friends, the tension
between them disappears—they enjoy talking to each other as long as
it is about themselves. They declare their feelings for each other.

Exhausted but happy, Nina spends most nights walking and
necking with Mitch—they can't seem to agree on anything else to do.
The first time they make love it doesn't go well. Nina blames herself,
and Mitch blames himself. They spend more and more time in Mitch's
apartment. Their lovemaking improves; they even read *The Joy of Sex*
together. Before long, they decide that since they are spending so
much time together, it makes sense for them to live together. So, on a
Saturday in December, Nina and Emmett move into Mitch's
apartment. One of the many conflicts between them is that Mitch does
not like the cat. Nina assumes that this and all the other differences
between them will disappear as they come to know each other by
living together.

Of course, the conflicts build and grow. At first living together is
fun, sort of like playing house. But soon little things begin to annoy
Nina about Mitch. She is surprised by the large degree of intimacy
involved in living together—not only because of the small space, but
trying to accommodate each other's routine as well. Nina also begins
to worry about her parents finding out about their living together.

Nina and Mitch continue to see Sonia and the beautiful, unhappy
Lynell. The relationships between Nina's ex-roommates and their
boyfriends are frequently a topic of discussion. Lynell's boyfriend lies
to her and continues to see other girls, another foreshadowing of
events to come. Nina begins working for the wonderful Professor
Lehman. One day, needing to confide in someone, she unexpectedly
tells Professor Lehman about her living arrangements with Mitch.
Nina feels sorry for him because his wife has left him and he misses
his little daughter. She imagines that he is wishing he were twenty
again:

> They were flirting. She was flirting; so was he. Her face
> was warm; she couldn't stop smiling. The way he was

looking at her . . . and his eyes were so *blue*. They were
like blue lights. He lit his pipe, looking at her over the
stem. When she began typing again, her hands were moist.
(119)

After the vacation, Mitch's and Nina's arguments escalate. She is
beginning to suspect that something is not right between the two of
them and Nina believes he is keeping a distance between them. Her
intuition turns out to be correct—within a few months it becomes clear
that Mitch has been seeing Lynell.

Nina, too, is unfaithful to Mitch. One Sunday afternoon Professor
Lehman calls and asks Nina to come to his house to do some typing.
Over Mitch's objections she goes, saying that he has a deadline to
meet on his book. That afternoon Professor Lehman kisses her for the
first time. She is still an observer in her own life and Nina finds
herself thinking about him even while she is kissing Mitch.

One afternoon, Nina's conflict with Mitch over the cat comes to a
climax. Mitch lets Emmett get out when he is opening the door to let
Lynell in. Later that evening Nina finds Emmett dead in a gutter
where he'd been thrown by a car. She takes the cat back to the
apartment, stiff with grief. Mitch is not there. When he comes back he
apologizes without any real compassion for her pain. But Nina is not
convinced that he and Lynell did not let the cat out on purpose. When
Mitch suggests that they put Emmett's body in the garbage, Nina
refuses angrily. They bury him and with that, though they do not
know it yet, they also bury their relationship.

Shortly after Emmett's death, Professor Lehman comforts Nina.
They make love on a rug in his house:

> *Hold me, comfort me . . . Please comfort me.* He was
> holding her. Couldn't he hold her tighter? She burrowed
> into him, to be close and comforted. They were falling
> down on the rug, falling, falling, falling . . . close, close,
> close . . . She heard someone crying, little mewing sounds,
> oh, oh, oh, it was her. . . . And all this was mixed with
> tears. (230)

Things continue to get worse between Nina and Mitch. He is out
of a job and depressed. Nina stops working for Professor Lehman and
even begins cutting his class, but finally, afraid she might fail, she
goes back. She is still attracted to him. Following class he calls her to

his office, and he asks whether she thinks the lovemaking was voluntary. We get the sense that Nina is not the first vulnerable coed he has seduced. She tells him it wasn't his "fault." He retorts that he didn't know that word was in her generation's vocabulary. She is hurt and angry. It's as if she wasn't there—didn't have anything to do with the lovemaking. He kisses her and closes the door to the office:

> "No," she said. "No, I can't. I can't do . . . that again. I won't." And she ran. The door banged behind her. Down the empty corridor she ran, her footsteps clattering. God, oh, God, had she said it; had she done it? Humiliated, relieved, she ran all the way home, shaking with reckless laughter. (242)

This is our first inkling that Nina, like most of Mazer's female characters, has self-respect and strength.

It is spring and although things seem a little better between Mitch and Nina, they still keep secrets from each other. Nina's tryst with Nicholas Lehman was her acknowledgment of the approaching end of her relationship with Mitch. She tells Mitch she has made love with the professor, but that it was only one time. He, trying to hurt her too, tells her he did it with Lynell anytime she was willing. They stay together, perhaps because they do not know any alternative. At the end of the school year, it is clear that they will not live together again in the fall. The relationship is over; like Seth and Finn, they will each go their separate ways.

As in *Up in Seth's Room*, the relationship between Nina and Mitch ends because they are not ready to make the commitment that intimacy demands. They, like Seth and Finn, are far too self-centered to give fully to another person. They use each other to meet their mutual need for someone to love.

Although Nina grows in the novel, she does not have the strength of character of Mazer's other female protagonists. Mitch seems to change very little during the course of the story, and the seducing Professor Lehman changes not at all.

Someone to Love, although a tantalizing story, reads like an answer to some of the criticism of *Up in Seth's Room*. Mazer seems to be saying to her critics, "I, too, can write a young adult novel in which the characters have intercourse." Not surprisingly, most critics of young adult books responded positively to it. Critic Eaglen suggests that "sex is an essential part of the relationship between Nina and

Mitch but it is not explicit. Altogether this is an honest and touching look at a bittersweet youthful love affair."[6] Mary K. Chelton writes in *Voice of Youth Advocates*, *Someone to Love* is a "useful book beyond casual reading for freshman orientations in colleges, values discussions in teen sexuality rap sessions, and high school guidance offices."[7] Interestingly, Mazer dedicated this novel to one of her closest literary friends, the late Norma Klein, whose novels frequently broke literary taboos.

Other Short Romances

Among Norma Fox Mazer's short stories there are several romances that illustrate her considerable literary skills. Mazer again explores the topic of a strong girl refusing to have sex in the short story "What Happened in the Cemetery," published in *Nineteen: Short Stories by Outstanding Writers for Young Adults*, edited by Donald Gallo.

Fan agrees to go to the cemetery with Richie—even though she knows why kids go to the cemetery—just so it will happen. They barely know each other. The encounter is a disaster, but from it Fan learns what Nina fails to: sex without caring is not fulfilling.

In "Up on Fong Mountain," which appears in the 1976 book *Dear Bill, Remember Me?*, the students in a high school English class are required to keep a journal. At first Jessie resents this assignment—she has nothing to write about and her journal shows her lack of enthusiasm. However, soon she meets B.D. and the rest of her journal chronicles their up-and-down romance.

In the title story of the book, "Dear Bill, Remember Me?," Kathy writes to Bill, who was her older sister's boyfriend. Bitsy has always had a crush on him. When she sees the announcement of his marriage in the paper she tries to tell him, through a series of letters she never sends, what he meant to her.

"Avie Loves Ric Forever" and "Summer Girls, Love Boys" were both published in the book *Summer Girls, Love Boys and Other Short Stories* in 1982. In "Avie Loves Ric Forever," Richie writes love letters to Stevie. She and Stevie have been childhood friends. Now they are older and she thinks he will never see her in the romantic light in which she sees him. AVIE LOVES RIC FOREVER is painted in Day-Glo above an overpass. One day, walking under the overpass, Richie

sees in Day-Glo paint: STAVIE LOVES RICH FOREVER. Stevie has
added three letters and in those letters he tells Richie how he really
feels about her.

"Summer Girls, Love Boys" tells the story of Mary Lewisham the
summer she was fifteen, cut her hair, and met Bobby Nicholes. Mazer
uses haircutting in several of her works. In *Someone to Love* Nina cuts
off her braids because they make her look too young. According to
Mazer, haircutting is a symbolic gesture:

> She's coming out from behind the masks, facing the world
> still with fear, but bravely. Maybe the way we all face the
> world. This haircutting goes back to when I was thirteen
> and my older sister cut my hair. I'll never forget going to
> school the next day and hearing several classmates say, "I
> didn't recognize you!" That was wonderful for me. It was
> what I wanted—to be transformed, not really be someone
> else, but to be different than I was. Don't all adolescents
> long for transformation?[8]

When We First Met

If *Someone to Love* is Mazer's simplest romance, *When We First
Met*, written a year earlier in 1982, is the most complex. We first came
to know its protagonist, Jenny Pennoyer, in the 1973 novel *A Figure of
Speech*. The premise of the novel, its spine, is quite simple. Jenny
meets Rob, the boy of her dreams, who turns out to be the son of the
woman who killed Jenny's younger sister while driving drunk. She
can't imagine life without Rob, but feels torn in many directions when
she finds out who he is. The flesh and blood of this novel, the
characters, are carefully developed and well drawn. We come to know
not only Jenny and Rob, but his mother and her parents. We did not
get to know the senior Pennoyers as real people in *A Figure of Speech*.
(This novel will be discussed in chapter seven.) As reviewer Mary
Lystad writes in *Children's Writers*, in *When We First Met*
"relationships are complex, often explosive, and they ring true."[9] A
reviewer in the *Bulletin of the Center for Children's Books* praises the
novel for "its insight into the complexity of attitudes and emotions in

the characters, all of whom are drawn with depth and compassion in a story with good narrative flow and natural dialogue."[10]

Mazer says of her writing that she's "very conscious of the connection of memory to story."[11] However, when she first began *When We First Met* she was not sure how it connected to her life. The bare bones of the story, its spine, seemed totally removed from her experience. However, the more she wrote, the more she remembered the fear of nearly being hit by a car while riding her bike as an adolescent and a near miss when running out into the road after a ball as a child. She can imagine Gail's terror and the pain and guilt experienced by the Pennoyers, particularly Jenny, after Gail's death.

Far more than a story of forbidden love, *When We First Met* is a tale of hate and forgiveness. In the pages of the novel, Mazer asks and attempts to answer many questions: When is it possible to forgive even if we can't forget? Should a drunk driver ever be forgiven? What happens when our enemy has a face, a life, feelings? How does hate affect our lives and the lives of those we love? When can we begin to live again after the tragic death of a loved one?

Critic C. Nordhielm Wooldridge writes of *When We First Met*, "This is basically an updated and freshly inspired Romeo and Juliet story: a young couple pitted against a spiteful, vindictive older generation. Shakespeare buffs may sniff at the untragic ending but most readers will heave a satisfied sigh when the plot takes the one final twist that allows these 'star-crossed lovers' to work things out."[12]

This is a novel that sings to the soul. It is far more than a love story—although it is a fine romance. It is a novel that speaks to the heart and to the intellect. At the end of the novel we cannot answer the questions that have been posed throughout. We do not know how much retribution should be required, nor do we know how much pain can be endured. We do not know who was right and who wrong. However, Mazer has made it clear without beating us over the head with it—healing must occur or life will never again be normal, happy. This is Mazer's best romance. In fact, it is one of the finest romance novels in young adult literature.

Notes

1. Jean Fritz, review of *Up in Seth's Room*, *New York Times Book Review* (January 20, 1980): 30.
2. Norma Fox Mazer, *"Up in Seth's Room*: Some Thoughts," *The ALAN Review* (Fall 1980): 1.
3. Patty Campbell, review of *Up in Seth's Room*, *Wilson Library Bulletin* (October 1979): 123, 139.
4. Review of *Up in Seth's Room*, *Kirkus Reviews* (December 1979): 1380.
5. Review of *Up in Seth's Room*, *ALA Booklist* (November 1, 1979): 440.
6. Audrey B. Eaglen, review of *Someone to Love*, *School Library Journal* (Spring 1983): 137.
7. Mary K. Chelton, review of *Someone to Love*, *Voice of Youth Advocates* (October 1983): 206.
8. Norma Fox Mazer, "Growing Up with Stories," *Top of the News* (Winter 1985): 166.
9. Mary Lystad, review of *When We First Met*, *Twentieth-Century Children's Writers*. Chicago, IL: St. James Press (1989): 652.
10. Review of *When We First Met*, *Bulletin of the Center for Children's Books* (July-August, 1983): 214.
11. Mazer, "Growing Up," 165.
12. C. Nordhielm Woodridge, review of *When We First Met*, *School Library Journal* (February 1983): 91.

Chapter 4

Norma and Harry: Relationship, Romance, and Writing

It is impossible to write about Norma Fox Mazer without discussing her fifty-year relationship with Harry Mazer. Their long marriage is based on more than love and family; it is also built on respect and encouragement. In fact, it is a writing partnership as well as a marriage. Norma says that Harry is always the first reader of her manuscripts, and frequently during the writing process Harry helps Norma over hurdles. Harry claims that without Norma it is unlikely that he would be writing today. Not only did Norma encourage Harry to give up the jobs that supported the family in order to write, she supported him emotionally and at times financially during the long, arduous process of becoming a writer.

Norma met Harry when she was just fifteen and he was twenty-one. She remembers him as a tall, curly-haired, Air Force veteran. They met through her just-married older sister. When Norma returned home after meeting him, she told her best friend that she'd just met this incredibly handsome guy named Harry Mazer, "too bad he was so—ughhh-*old.*"[1] Two years later they met again; Norma was seventeen and Harry twenty-three, but somehow this time he didn't seem that much older. According to Norma she had to work really hard to get Harry to notice her because he thought she was too young.

Harry doesn't quite remember it that way. He remembers their *first* meeting vividly and used it, or aspects of it, in several of his novels. He came out from under a car on which he was working and saw Norma for the first time. (At one point Hilary, a character in the Mazers' joint novel *Heartbeat,* comes out from under a car and sees Tod.) She was beautiful. He had noticed her and knew right away he was interested in her. In fact that day he drove her sixty miles home and they talked about books the entire time. However, he does agree with her on one point: she was too young.

Two years later when they met again—this time at a political rally she was attending with her sister—Harry actively pursued the relationship. Not only were he and Norma both interested in books, they had the same politics. The rally was for third-party candidate Henry Wallace in the 1948 presidential campaign. Wallace lost the election to Harry Truman, but Harry Mazer won Norma's heart.

Norma and Harry were drawn together by their common interest in books and things literary. Harry and Norma had grown up in working-class families and were both idealists—believing in the power of the working man and in socialism. These kinds of beliefs were not radical in Norma's family. Norma came from a more bookish background than Harry—books were very important to her father and grandfather—but Harry had always loved books. Norma remembers how enlightened he seemed. Now she realizes that his sophistication came not from personal experience but from what he had read in books. He could talk about any topic and Norma was very impressed by his intelligence.

Although Norma entered college in Ohio, she only remained in school for a little more than a semester. She returned to New York to marry Harry. Norma was an eighteen-year-old college freshman and Harry was twenty-three. Harry admits that Norma was much too young for marriage. Norma's uncle tried to convince her not to marry the guy, but to just live with him. At the time she was insulted by the suggestion and didn't know if she could ever forgive her uncle—living with someone was unthinkable in 1950.

The first few months of their marriage were spent in New York

City, but Norma could not stand the noise and the dirt, so they moved to Schenectady. Norma remembers the first months of their marriage as a time of *talking* about books, writing, and literature. They also talked about "politics, unions, injustice, the atom bomb, the cold war."[2] According to Norma, they were radicals ready to reform (reform, says Norma) the world. They also were beginning a life together, making a home, learning to cook.

During the early years of their married life, Harry had many jobs as a laborer, and Norma had babies, working part-time as a cashier or a salesclerk. Harry was not only working to support his growing family, he was working to support his political beliefs. Norma kept dreaming of becoming a writer. When they had three children under six, Norma would keep a pad in her jeans pocket and write down clever things the kids said. At the time, Anne was about five, Joey was two, and Susan was an infant. Even when their children were this young, Norma and Harry found time to talk and to walk. They were living in Syracuse's First Ward, the first settled part of town. They'd walk around the old section and dream together. They'd stop and buy bread at an Italian bakery and pick the mushrooms that grew up in the cracks of the sidewalks.

They both knew Norma wanted to become a writer—she'd known since she was thirteen but she was surprised when Harry started talking about writing as well. She guesses that she probably should have recognized the signs. He had been talking for some time about how unhappy he was with his work, and she knew that he had been keeping notebooks—always had kept notebooks. However, Harry has always been the quieter of the two—working out his thoughts and his problems internally, whereas Norma formulates her thoughts while talking and writing.

Norma, they both agree, is also the first one to take action. Harry claims that she has a type A personality, while his is a type Z. She calls herself practical. And so Norma decided that if they both wanted to be writers they should do something about it. They should write every day to begin to form a writing habit. Every night after the children were in bed, they'd sit across from each other at an old oak table with notebooks and pens and write for an hour. They stuck to this schedule for about three years. She wonders how they found time to write between, work, kids, talking, and dreaming.

When Norma was pregnant with their fourth child and Harry was frustrated with the menial nature of his jobs, having lost a teaching job and been denied another because of his political beliefs, they began writing full time. It started when Norma would wake up very early in the morning, restless because of her pregnancy, and write. She suggested to Harry that rather than writing at night after a long day at work and with the children, he should do the same. He began getting up with her at 3:30 a.m. and writing for two to three hours before the day began. They did this for almost a year. During this time Gina was born. It is hard to imagine how tired they must have been at the end of every day, but they were both finding their efforts at writing rewarding. Each of them had sold a few things. They were not making much money, but they could see how it would be possible to make a living as freelance writers—neither of them required many material things.

It was an unexpected settlement from a car accident Norma had had a few years earlier—twenty-five hundred dollars—that made their dream a reality. Gina was two months old; they had four children under ten, and Harry quit his job in the factory. Figuring they could live six months on twenty-five hundred dollars, they began writing every day. Norma reports being terrified, some days sitting in front of the typewriter shaking because she couldn't think what to write next.

Although they do not speak of it in this way, they were savvy business people. They knew that in order to feed their family they each had to sell one piece of writing per week. In those days, magazines paid by the word—two to five cents. Therefore a five-thousand-word story would sell for one hundred to two hundred and fifty dollars. They analyzed the market and decided that the women's romance and confession magazines were steady and reliable, and needed plenty of stories. Norma reports that "despite the lurid titles, [romances] were stories of relationships: men and women, parents and children, brothers and sisters. Someone—the narrator or the chief character— made a mistake, did something wrong, 'sinned.' Every action had a reaction, a consequence. The world of these stories was strict and moral."[3] Norma and Harry knew they could learn how to write romance stories and could write them quickly.

Early on they got in the habit of writing seven days a week. These years of producing pulp fiction taught them both how to write. They read other writers and read about writing, but mostly they wrote, figuring out how to craft stories as they went. According to Norma, writing story after story forced her "to learn how a story is constructed, how to hold a reader's attention, how to write dialogue and narration, how to do simple, yet previously baffling things like transitions."[4] With the large number of stories they were writing without a byline, it was not unusual to pick up a confession magazine and find three or more stories from one or the other of them. They were making a living at writing—at one time, nearly $30,000 a year between them. They were happy, but they were not totally fulfilled.

They both wanted to write a novel, but were trapped in their own version of catch-22. To support the family, they needed to write one story per week; to write a novel, they needed their writing time to focus on the novel. Somehow, however, they pieced together the time to each write a novel. Both Norma's first, *I, Trissy,* and Harry's first, *Guy Lenny,* were published in 1971. They had been writing professionally for nearly ten years by that time.

Norma remembers an incident two years later that was both "funny and heartbreaking." Her second book, *A Figure of Speech,* was nominated for the National Book Award. One of the committee members said to her, " . . . and you just came out of nowhere."[5] She laughed and smiled graciously, but thought to herself that her "nowhere" was a ten-year apprenticeship writing un-bylined pulp fiction stories for magazines. It was that hard work that taught her how to write in first person, as she does in *I, Trissy,* how to write in the voice of a variety of different protagonists, and, most importantly, how to tell a good story.

The Relationship

You can't be around Norma and Harry Mazer for long without knowing how important they are to each other. The strength of their relationship and the strength of Norma herself helps to explain her strong female characters and her ability to write from a male perspective. And their enduring relationship of equals also makes it clear why strong female characters are central to so many of Harry's novels. In fact, they each credit themselves with helping the other gain these skills. Norma says it is because of her that Harry developed his first strong female protagonist, Cindy in *Snow Bound* (Harry's second novel, published in 1973). In the first draft, Cindy's only response to being stranded in a snowbound car on a deserted plateau was to cry. Norma, who always is the first reader of Harry's drafts, did not worry about hurting his feelings. She simply told him that Cindy didn't work as a character in an adventure story—she needed to be as strong as Tony and she needed to defeat the environment with Tony. Of course, Norma was right.

However, Norma is not always right. She tells a funny tale she calls "the-not-me-before-you-Honey story." Prior to the publication of their first novels, Norma told Harry that she would never publish first. She says with a sheepish twinkle, "I thought I needed to protect his male ego." The answer to the question of whose novel was really published first depends on whom you ask. Norma says that both her first novel, *I, Trissy,* and Harry's first novel, *Guy Lenny,* were published on the exact same day. Harry, on the other hand, claims that Norma's novel was published before his.

The Writers

One of the things that make Norma and Harry Mazer unique as writers and as a couple is that they write both alone and together. They are not the only team of married writers in the young adult market— Vera and Bill Cleaver wrote together for many years. Other teams also exist in the field of young adult books. The brothers James Lincoln Collier and Christopher Collier are well known for their historical fiction, for example, and professors Lee Irwin and Ann Hadley wrote under the combined name Hadley Irwin.

However, Harry Mazer and Norma Fox Mazer were for many years a married couple who individually wrote successful young adult novels. They talk about their union being a literary marriage, initially based on their common interest in reading and later their common interest in writing. According to Harry, it is "first a marriage in fact and then a marriage in fancy."[6]

Harry and Norma are very different in terms of their approach to writing. She is inner driven. She gets up in the morning and begins writing immediately. If she doesn't, she is very restless and unhappy. Harry, on the other hand, is more likely to do other things first. In fact, he talks about his need to write the book in his head before he puts it on paper—or now, the word processor. However, Norma says that

Harry has a "freer personality." She says that he is "more adventurous and willing to break out than I am—in a lot of ways, in doing things and in writing as well." She says that she talks about breaking out— would like to be more adventurous—but when she sits down to write she is always doing what she always does. Then she admits, "but I like what I do. I enjoy it. I love it. I love writing about relationships, but I still would like to do something else, but I find it very difficult. I think, in that sense, Harry has more range than I do." Here, as is often the case, Norma is underestimating her ability. She writes in numerous genres: realistic fiction, suspense, mystery, science fiction, and historical fiction. This certainly is an indication that she, too, has a large range. She writes in many voices: children, adolescents, parents, unmarried adults, the elderly, male, female, and eccentrics of varying kinds. She can even change point of view and person several times during a single novel. She utilizes numerous literary techniques: journal writing, letter writing, narrative, dialogue, stream of con- sciousness, and poetry. And, most importantly, she always tells a good story that keeps readers turning the pages. There are few writers who can do all of this and do it as well as Norma Fox Mazer.

Of course, two writers living together isn't always easy. Writers argue a lot. They're sensitive. They need a lot of praise. They need to be petted. They need to be told what they've written is good. They're full of doubts and never sure that what they've done is good enough, and when one is a type A and the other is a type Z, it can be awfully hard.

Harry maintains that Norma is more helpful to his writing than he is to her writing. She disagrees, "Well, I don't think that's true. I think we really help each other a lot. I know that when I'm working I'm just a mess of anxieties. I am worried and have insecurities about 'am I doing this right?' I know he thinks the same things. . . . It is very nice to know that someone you can trust will read it for you."

Although, Norma reports that her confidence as a writer has grown significantly and she is no longer fearful that she has nothing to say, she still responds with difficulty to Harry's criticism, even though she knows he is almost always correct. This happened again when Norma completed her fourth or fifth draft of *When She Was Good*. This magnificent novel, published in 1997, had been very difficult for her to write. In fact, she did not show it to Harry immediately following drafting it as she typically does—she waited until just before she planned to send it to her publisher. Harry read it silently. She could tell by the expression on his face that something was wrong. He knew how long and hard she had been working on it and was reluctant to criticize it. However, when he finally told her his opinion, she was devastated. He told her it was too hard—that there was no hope in the novel. It took Norma a few days to recover from his remarks, but when she did she sat down to write the final draft. The story is still hard, but there is hope, and, Harry was right, the hope makes the story a remarkable tale of strength, character, and love.

In spite of her anger at Harry, Norma recognizes the importance of his criticism. She says that he helps her to be more adventurous while she helps him strengthen the relationships in his books. Norma depends a great deal on Harry's literary opinions. "I really trust his judgment," she says with emphasis. "Although sometimes he tries to cut too much," she laughs. Harry also trusts Norma's reactions, but complains that she always wants him to expand his work too much.

In the end, they both also recognize how important they are to each other—each of them giving the other credit for his or her impact on the novels, even the ones they write alone. It is a joy simply listening to the two of them talk—playing with new ideas, sharing thoughts about their work, and examining the processes they use. Their harmonious bantering back and forth—completing each other's thoughts and working through to solutions—has helped each of them in all stages of their writing.

The Team

In 1977 Harry and Norma wrote their first novel together—*The Solid Gold Kid*. Shortly after its completion they agreed they would never do another together. It was more than ten years before they published *Heartbeat*, their second joint work, in 1989. Then, only three years later, they published *Bright Days, Stupid Nights*.

I had a conversation with Norma about how two such different personalities write as a team. "It's a real push-pull," she says. We really fight sometimes because we do write differently and we do have a different take [on things]. At its best, we are adding to each other. We are both giving our strengths."

"And, at its worst?" I ask her. She hesitates for some time, laughs, stumbles over her words, and laughs again, "At its worst, we're really close to divorce." She admits that they frequently joke about writing together. She recalls telling me and other people shortly after *The Solid Gold Kid* came out, "I'll never write with that man again!" But, she can't remember exactly why they found it so difficult to work together. Harry comes up with most of the ideas and "the stuff," and because she has a more complete sense of what the finished manuscript will look like, Norma links his pieces together. "That's my strength," she says, "I want things to link together. Well, he does too, but I can do that better than he does."

The collaboration for each of their three joint novels has been slightly different—in part due to different technology, in part due to particular circumstance, and in part due to conscious changes they have made.

The Solid Gold Kid was originally Harry's story. Harry had written the first draft of the book, but Norma did not like the characters. And, as she says, "It was in the drawer." They decided to pull it out of the drawer because it had a lot of plot and movement, something they knew they needed for a joint novel. Norma took the draft and started working on the characters. She can't remember whether after this Harry took it back again or they simply worked on it together until it was completed. She does remember, though, that it was written on an old manual typewriter, and by the time they were done each page was many pieces cut and stapled together. It was double and triple spaced so that there was room to cross out and make changes.

Norma and Harry smile at each other as they describe working on revisions of the novel at their camp in Canada while they were building their rustic cabin. As with all of her novels and most of Harry's, Norma has a clear sense of where it was written and revised. They recall a photograph of the two of them sitting at a table at their summer camp working on the manuscript of *The Solid Gold Kid* with carpentry tools in the background. Norma reports that building their "little bunkhouse" was nearly as difficult as writing the book together—maybe this added to the problem of writing the book. According to Norma, she'd never built anything before—never handled tools. She says that she learned a whole lot about tools and building, but even more about feeling dumb and insufficient.

Harry did the first draft of all of their joint books. The second and third novels they intended to be joint works from the beginning. Norma says that after Harry drafts, she has permission to go in and do anything she wants to it. Today they write and revise their manuscripts, individually and jointly, on a computer:

> We edit on the computer. I know some people print out . . . . What I usually do is either work in capital letters or underline it, or something. I'll just make suggestions . . .
> If I think he's over-written, I'll put an 'X' in front of the phrase or the word or something like that. But no, I wouldn't [wipe it out]. Or, if I wanted to do that I would create another file so that I wouldn't touch the original. I'm very antsy about anybody touching my work. I mean, I listen to Harry, although it's very hard for me still. I hate it when he criticizes my writing. I recognize that probably ninety-nine percent of the time it's justified.

Harry breaks in and explains how they have begun working jointly at the computer. He says that while Norma is sitting at the keyboard and he's sitting next to her and they have a problem, he'll "murmur something—sort of a half-formed idea, and she'll take it and develop it a little bit more. Then I find it's wonderful," Harry says, "because it's almost like a duet."

When they wrote *Heartbeat*, their second joint novel, they talked the whole book out first and then Harry wrote the first draft. Then Norma took the draft and tore it to pieces and put it back together. That's when the conflicts started. When it was his turn with the manuscript Norma told him, "Don't you dare touch a word."[7] I asked Norma if it had really happened this way. "It probably did," she laughed, "it sounds like something I would say."

Then they worked on the manuscript together—several times. They sat side by side at the computer, fighting over lines. This caused a lot of tension because their writing styles are so different. According to Harry, "I want to condense everything while Norma wants to expand every idea." Norma agrees with Harry on this point; she says that it's one of the ways she helps him. She remembers that when he wrote *I Love You, Stupid!* they were at their camp in Canada. She was reading and saying, "Tell me more; it's not enough." Harry would start talking and Norma would write down what he was saying—helping him think through what he wanted to write.

As they wrote and revised *Heartbeat* they had "constant disagreements, long silences, heavy sighs, [and] deep breathing," recalls Harry. Usually Norma and Harry negotiate their way through their arguments. They each listen to see if the other person has a valid point and if their personal ideas should not be held on to so strongly. Norma sometimes says, "You give a little," and sometimes Norma finds herself thinking, "Maybe he's right. Maybe this is excessive. Maybe there *are* too many words."

The Solid Gold Kid

The Solid Gold Kid, the Mazers' first joint novel, provides a good example of how Harry has helped Norma become more adventurous, and how Norma has helped Harry improve his characters and their relationships. The novel is both a story about relationships and a tale of suspense. Derek, the protagonist, has almost no contact with his divorced parents, has few friends at his boarding school, and desperately wants to meet a pretty blonde girl he sees on his way to the bus stop one rainy Saturday afternoon. His desire to meet her inadvertently puts both of them and several other young people into the midst of a kidnapping plot to abduct Derek, whose father is one of the wealthiest men in the country. Reviews, although mixed, have found the story to be fast-paced and exciting—Harry's contribution—and the characters to be "developed with empathy and understanding"[8]—which is Norma's.

Heartbeat

The Mazers' second joint novel was published more than a decade after their first. *Heartbeat* is about an unusual love triangle between three young people. Tod is handsome but shy, and has never had a girlfriend. His more gregarious friend Amos, who once saved Tod's life following a swimming accident, is short, cute, and funny. Amos falls for Hilary and asks Tod to return his life-saving favor as he has promised. Tod reluctantly agrees to talk to Hilary for Amos. And he really does try. Not unpredictably, however, Tod and Hilary fall in love. Tod doesn't know how to tell Amos of his and Hilary's involvement.

Although the plot is a typical love triangle, borrowed from *Cyrano de Bergerac* or John Alden in *The Courtship of Miles Standish*, it expands beyond the formula when Amos is hospitalized with a viral infection that has permanently weakened his heart. As the friends learn that Amos may not survive, Tod tells Hilary of his promise and deception. Hilary decides to pretend that she is in love with Amos while he is in the hospital. Tod feels both guilt and jealousy and, not surprisingly, Hilary does come to love Amos. After his death, it is clear to both Tod and Hilary that they can't go back to the way they had been before.

Many reviewers, including Jack Forman, discussed the "strong, nonsterotypical characterization."[9] Reviewer Trish Ebbatson suggests that the strength of the story "lies in the characters' relationships with each other, their feelings of obligation and commitment, and an understanding of when the needs of the others take priority."[10]

Harry's crafting of plot can also be seen in the novel. As Zena Sutherland suggests, "It's a moving story, psychologically intricate and convincing, that explores the conflict between romantic love and loyalty to a friend in a way that is broader than the immediate situation of the story."[11] Reviewers also call it "fast-paced" (Sutherland) with a "strong narrative sense [that] keeps the reader engaged" (Ebbatson).

Heartbeat is a joint novel that allows us to see the team of Norma Fox Mazer and Harry Mazer at their best. The characters are well drawn and realistic. They avoid the stereotypes of typical teenage romances. Each of the multidimensional characters seem to be the opposite of what appearance suggests.

The novel is told from Tod's point of view. This allows us to feel his frustration, fear, awkwardness, caring, and guilt. We come to really care about what happens to him. It is Harry's ability to develop a clear voice—a voice that is authentic—that makes Tod such a strong character.

Several chapters throughout the novel, printed in italics, are told from Hilary's point of view, written in first person. Those told from Tod's point of view are written in third. Harry recalls that he tried this technique in *Snow Bound*—having Tony tell the story in first person and Cindy in third. In this way, he believed their voices would be clearly distinguished. It didn't work, however, and he finally wrote it entirely in third person. Norma, too, changes point of view within novels, notably in *When We First Met*, but she does not attempt to change the person in which she tells that story.

Both Norma and Harry, alone and together, have continued to experiment with changing viewpoints. Even as they are working on a novel they change the viewpoint from first to third person, thereby adding another layer to the character. Harry admits that he has even changed a character's gender to see how the different point of view will affect dialogue, attitude, and emotion. He has done this "sex change" in the work he and Norma did for confession magazines, their "pulp work," as Harry calls it. Norma suggests that if you think about how your character would change by altering the gender, even if you do not do so in the novel, you add depth. Harry agrees. Perhaps this is why both Norma's and Harry's male and female characters are so realistic, sympathetic, and authentic.

Tod's difficult relationship with his father, another trademark of Harry's novels, adds to the interesting fabric of the work and adds another dimension to Tod's character. The creation of subplots that serve as a counterpoint or parallel to the main plot is a mark of Norma's work. As in both Norma's and Harry's other novels, the characters come to understand that there is far more to life than sex and even romantic love. As Tod realizes this he releases Hilary to help his friend Amos while he is dying. But his feelings are conflicted. He loves Hilary and cares deeply about Amos. He feels guilt about their deception and jealousy about Amos's and Hilary's relationship. At the same time, he knows he must attempt to save Amos's life as Amos had saved his. The moment at the end of the novel in which Amos draws Tod's and Hilary's hands together, a scene Norma fought to remove because she thought it seemed contrived, lets us know that Amos has not been deceived. He recognizes Tod's love for Hilary and he accepts and understands Tod's tremendous act of friendship.

Bright Days, Stupid Nights

Bright Days, Stupid Nights is the most recent joint novel written by the Mazers. It is told from the perspective of precocious fourteen-year-old Vicki Barfield and independent dreamer Chris Georgiade. Joining them in the novel are two other summer interns on a Pulitzer

Prize-winning newspaper: talkative Elizabeth and poised Faith. Both are beautiful, rich, and sophisticated. Vicki, on the other hand, had to lie about her age to get the internship. And Chris had to come against his father's wishes.

Vicki, who looks older than her fourteen years, is the daughter of a single mother who has high expectations for her. She is encouraged to take the internship in spite of the fact that it means lying about her age. Although Vicki is fearful, her mother convinces her she must go.

Chris is much like both Norma and Harry as adolescents. His family is large and Greek. (Both Norma and Harry are children of immigrant parents.) His father (like both of the Mazers' fathers) is a laborer. Chris, however, wants to be a writer and go to college. His father disapproves and thinks he should find a "real job." (Harry and his father had a similar conflict when he was an adolescent.) Chris feels like a duck out of water in his home (just as both Harry and Norma did). Chris is not ashamed of his family, he just feels different from them. He wins the internship after submitting an essay on his family's peculiar habits, parts of which appear in the first chapter of the novel. When Chris's father says he must take a summer job and not accept the internship, Chris runs away and sends his acceptance without his father's permission.

Elizabeth and Faith, the other two interns, are intentionally mysterious. We learn about Elizabeth's family only from what she says about them, and we learn almost nothing about Faith's family until Vicki discovers stories about Faith's father in the newspaper's morgue. Whether or not Vicki should write an article about Faith and her family's questionable past of intrigue, wealth, and controversy is one of the ethical dilemmas of the novel. Does the public have a right to know? Do innocent people deserve protection from the media?

Vicki and Faith argue about whether the story should be written. Their argument nearly turns into a tragedy when the interns side with Faith and decide to teach Vicki a lesson by locking her in an old truck. Fearing that she will suffocate and die, Vicki kicks her foot through a window and escapes. Sounds she hears in the darkness make her remember incidents from her past—incidents that make us better understand Vicki and her need to succeed and be recognized.

Vicki runs away after returning to the house to pack her things. With nowhere to go and no one to turn to, she decides to call Chris. They go to a diner and argue about whether she should return to Scottsville. Vicki says that everyone hates her. Chris replies:

> "Vicki, it's not hate. You know how Faith feels. And Elizabeth wants to protect Faith. And I think that journalism should be put to better use, especially by somebody as talented as you. . . . The crux, Vicki, is that we hate what you want to do, not you." (172)

Underlying the entire novel is a romance—actually several romances. Vicki is in love with Chris, although it takes him the entire novel to realize it. Chris is in love with Elizabeth, but is constantly confronted with her talk about her boyfriend Ira.

Throughout the novel Chris is becoming less and less satisfied with working at the newspaper. He realizes that much of the work is boring and takes no talent. They run errands and write obituaries and cutlines for pictures; they do little real reporting. He thinks of himself as fictionalizing everything, but has no idea where he is going with his novel. Chris, like all of the interns, is trying to find himself apart from his family and is frustrated by the process.

Like both *Up in Seth's Room* and *Someone to Love*, this novel does not end with the girl in the arms of the boy who has finally realized he loves her. Instead, the characters have found friendship. They have discovered each other's limitations and strengths and have decided to remain friends. The Mazers use the same technique at the end of this novel as at the end of their other two joint novels—the characters write letters to each other, a technique Norma has perfected in her individual novels and short stories. These letters sum up the novel, perhaps a bit too neatly, and let readers decide what will occur next.

Reviewer Stephanie Zvirin suggests that the plot is "deliberate, rather slow," and it "drags," but that "the characters are, for the most part, distinct."[12] Zena Sutherland has a similar concern, calling the novel "a padded situation-exploration."[13] Although it is true that this novel does not have the suspense and excitement of *The Solid Gold Kid*, the characters are far better developed. This novel is a character study, more typical of most of the Mazers' individual novels, rather than a novel that focuses on plot and action.

Even when writing individually, Norma Fox Mazer and Harry Mazer are a team. They may write alone, but they talk about what they are going to write, read what the other has written, help each other limit or expand what has been written, criticize each other's work, and celebrate each other's successes. They are proud of their work alone and their work together—both realizing that they are fine writers individually, but their individual strengths help make each other's work better. As Harry says, he thinks of their best writing together as a "duet." It is a duet with fine harmony in both their marriage and their work.

Notes

1. Adele Sarkissian, ed. *Something About the Author Autobiography Series,* Vol. 1. (Gale Research Company, 1986): 195.
2. Sarkissian, *Something About the Author,* 195.
3. Sarkissian, *Something About the Author,* 198.
4. Sarkissian, *Something About the Author,* 196.
5. Sarkissian, *Something About the Author,* 198.
6. Harry Mazer, speech, ALAN Workshop, St. Louis, MO. Unpublished (November 1988).
7. Harry Mazer, speech.
8. Jack Forman, review of *The Solid Gold Kid, School Library Journal* (September 1977): 148.
9. Jack Forman, review, 148.
10. Trish Ebbatson, review of *Heartbeat, School Library Journal* (June 1989): 124.
11. Zena Sutherland, review of *Heartbeat, Bulletin of the Center for Children's Books* (July/August 1989): 124.
12. Stephanie Zvirin, review of *Bright Days, Stupid Nights, ALA Booklist* (June 15, 1992): 1826.
13. Zena Sutherland, review of *Bright Days, Stupid Nights, Bulletin of the Center for Children's Books* (May 1992): 242.

Chapter 5

Writing for Younger Readers

Norma Fox Mazer's first novel, *I, Trissy*, published in 1971, was a book for young readers—what today is called a chapter book. At the time Norma wrote *I, Trissy* she did not know this. All she knew is she was finally, after ten years of making a living writing pulp fiction for magazines, the author of a novel. When she finished the manuscript and mailed it off to her agent, who gave it to Delacorte Press, she was convinced that she would not hear about it again for many months, perhaps ever. But within a month the editors at Delacorte wrote to Norma, telling her they wanted to publish *I, Trissy*. Norma was amazed, but clearly they had recognized her potential in this first good, but not great, novel for young readers.

Norma frequently quotes the English critic and short story writer V. S. Pritchett when she reflects on her early days of wanting to write so much that it hurt. Long after the years when she and Harry snatched an hour of writing after the children were finally asleep, she read Pritchett's autobiography and realized that he was describing exactly her state of mind at that time. He says of himself as a young man, "I found I simply wanted to write anything. . . . I had read that one writes because one has something to say. I could not see that I had anything to say except that I was alive." He goes on, "I simply wanted to write two or three sentences even as banal as the advertisement on a

sauce bottle, and see them in print with my name beneath them."[1] Like
Pritchett, Norma "had nothing but a love of words and, from some
mysterious place, the will to keep trying." She says that she, too,
believed she had nothing worth saying, and this frightened her almost
to paralysis.

That was Norma's frame of mind when she wrote *I, Trissy*. By the
time her first novel was published, Norma had been writing and
publishing for almost ten years. But rarely did her work carry a byline.
She had written many stories in varied voices, but still no one knew
who she was, and she firmly believed she had nothing important to
say. What she had was a need to write—a need to write a novel on
which her name would appear. And, so, somehow, sandwiched in
between taking care of four young children, talking and dreaming with
husband Harry, and writing one story of about five thousand words per
week to help put food on the table, Norma wrote her first novel.

She did not know when she wrote *I, Trissy* that it was a ground-
breaking book in the field of young adult literature, a genre still in its
infancy in 1971. (Most scholars date the beginning of young adult
literature with the publication of S. E. Hinton's *The Outsiders* in
1968.) Only a few authors—Norma Klein and Judy Blume, for
example—were writing in the authentic voices of real adolescents.
Norma is not sure why the voice in her first novel was the voice of a
young adolescent. Perhaps it was because she was fulfilling an
adolescent dream to write. She had known she wanted to be a writer
since she was thirteen—and now she was writing and publishing. Or,
maybe it was because, as Norma herself suggests, becoming a
published writer was a way of rejecting common sense:

> It was in some ways like a reversion to adolescence: the
> dream and the belief in the dream springing up fresh as a
> flower in my heart . . . Yes, definitely, I was an adolescent
> again, in love with writing, in a fever of desire, doing
> crazy things like getting up at 3:30 a.m. to write and
> neglecting important, grown-up things like housework.[2]

I, Trissy

What makes *I, Trissy* a good book is the seeds of excellence that
are planted in it. In her first novel, Norma includes many of the

important literary elements and techniques that she perfects in her later, more mature and accomplished works.

Her protagonist is well developed and has an authentic adolescent voice. Trissy is a plucky preteen, vulnerable, but strong. Although some critics call her "obnoxious" and "a brat," most recognize her as a "passionate, believable" heroine.[3]

The book employs a technique that Norma uses more effectively in later novels and short stories. The novel is written totally in Trissy's voice through a journal and letters she writes on her manual typewriter—probably the only thing that dates the novel.

The plot is a good one that Norma explores in many future books. Trissy's parents are splitting up, and she is responding to their problems with frustration and anger. As literary critic Sally Holmes Holtz suggests, Trissy's "spirited, indignant reactions, if not socially correct, seem reasonable, given her character. Readers who vicariously enjoy Trissy's sometimes outrageous behavior are witnessing a human being reacting to and adjusting to her situation and one who is eventually strong enough to accept that her parents will not get together again."[4]

The scene most reviewers cite, declaring Trissy to be either a brat, high-spirited, or a normal adolescent dealing with a troubling problem, is one in which she smears a cake her father's girlfriend has baked for him all over his apartment:

> I plunged both hands into the cake, all ten fingers. The cake was still warm inside. I squeezed and mashed it until it was all over the table top. Then I gathered gobs of chocolate fudge frosting in my hands. I smeared hand prints of frosting on the kitchen walls, through the livingroom, and out into the hall. Maybe I was laughing when I did it. Maybe I was crying. I thought, *Boy, this sure is a disgusting mess,* but I couldn't stop. I even smeared fudge frosting on the bannister going down the stairs. Then I walked home. 57 blocks. (121)

This short novel also has an interesting subplot. Trissy has a best friend, Steffi. Like the best friend relationships in many of Norma's novels for young readers, this one is challenged by the problems in Trissy's life. Her breakup with Steffi is a parallel to the separation of her parents.

Trissy gets involved in one unreasonable incident after another.
Every time she is remorseful. After she sets a fire in the wastebasket in
her room, trying to get rid of some of the things of her childhood—a
clear attempt to extricate herself from her situation and a cry for
help—she writes in her journal about how it makes her feel:

1. Hard for me to breathe.
2. As if a rock was pressed down on my chest.
3. Stupid and sorry.
4. Dumber than dumb.
5. Tired. Wished I could get into bed, pull the
covers over my head, and never come out. (136)

It is the incident of the fire that alerts both of her parents to
Trissy's true feelings—to her desperation. Even though she is
punished, her mother holds her in her arms and says to her, "My poor
baby . . . It hasn't been easy for you, has it, Trissy?" (137). Her father
phones, saying that no matter what he and her mother decide to do she
will always be Trissy Jane Beers, that's who she was born, and they
will always love her. He tells her not to cry, "We all make mistakes,
and yours are just childish ones" (141).

As in all of Norma's novels, Trissy grows up during the telling of
the story. Although her new maturity does not have the depth of the
maturation of later protagonists, such as Jenny Pennoyer in *When We
First Met*, she makes up with her friend Steffi and starts putting her
energy into more positive things like becoming the editor of the school
paper.

Norma has every right to be proud of *I, Trissy*. Her readers have
told her that they understand Trissy—that she is one with them. A girl
from Chicopee, Massachusetts, wrote to Norma:

> Trissy and I are very similar. Our parents are divorced, we
> have problems with our brothers . . . We both have fights
> with our friends and both our parents have either a
> girlfriend or a boyfriend.[5]

Her readers have also told her that the novel has stood the test of
time. Kate from Allentown, Pennsylvania, wrote to Norma, "*I, Trissy*
was handed down to me by my older sister, Amy . . ."[6]

In *I, Trissy* we see Norma's enormous literary potential. Her
second novel, *A Figure of Speech* (1974), and her third novel,

Saturday, the Twelfth of October (1975), are far more complex and intricate than *I, Trissy*. They, too, are for young adolescent readers. When Norma wrote *Dear Bill, Remember Me?* (1976), her first book of short stories, she began to write for a more mature adolescent audience. In fact, most of the books that followed her first short story collection are for older readers.

Norma says that while she was writing *Dear Bill, Remember Me?* she began to believe for the first time that she was really a writer—that she had something to say. The voice she was finding was in more mature adolescent characters. This may be because the lives of older adolescents are typically more intense, and more mature readers can handle more intricate plots with more hard-hitting and important themes. Or it might be, as Norma suggests, she was growing up. Although this older, more mature voice continued in most of her later work, in the mid-1980s Norma began a series of books for younger readers.

The A-B-C, Best Friend Novels

Norma, from her earliest years as a published writer, has followed publishing trends. By the early 1980s it was clear that the series book was taking over the young adult market. Norma, like many writers and critics, was concerned that most of these books had stories that were too predictable and characters that were wooden. She has long believed that children need good books.

Norma expressed her concern in "Bread, Books, and Passion," an article for the International Reading Association journal *Signal*, that the books kids were exposed to were not real bread, not real books— they were series books, formula books. They were products not created passionately by their authors, but were instead "hacked out for the market and for no other reason."[7] This was harsh criticism of the publishing industry and it is still echoed today by many authors, reviewers, and critics of children's and young adult books.

Norma is not someone to criticize what children read. She herself had been a reader of many things, from *Gulliver's Travels* to *Pollyanna* to Nancy Drew. Additionally, she had read her parent's books. Although she didn't always understand them, the act of reading—of finding the story—was pure pleasure. In her own childhood home there were no comics, but she could cross the street to Buddy Wells's house and read *Wonder Woman* or *Elastic Man*.

When her own children were young, Norma decided that everything would be available in their home—even comics. She does admit that when her son Joey became an avid comic book reader— with books stacked to the top of his closet—she had to resist the temptation to throw them away. She leafed through them and was angered by how "lurid, violent, racist, and sexist" they were.[8] However, she has long held to the belief that "no printed word, sentence, or story ever killed or maimed anyone, that reading leads to more reading, and that, finally, given time, the kids would develop their own tastes which, hopefully, would include much more than comics."[9] This has certainly been the case with her children. As adults all of them are avid readers, and Anne has followed in her parents' footsteps and is an accomplished, critically acclaimed children's book author.

So, Norma does not criticize what children choose to read. Nor does she suggest that formulaic series books should not be published. Instead, she makes a case for authoring and publishing books that older children and young adolescents can "get their teeth into."

Norma addresses the issue of formulaic books written by hired-hand writers in two of her best friend novels. The irony of dealing with this issue in a series novel is not lost on mature readers. In the second novel in the series, *B, My Name Is Bunny*, Bunny writes to the author of a favorite series book. Bunny is an avid reader who passes her books on to her best friend, Emily. In the letter she congratulates the author on his "great talent for writing"—there is no accounting for the taste of kids. However, what she is most interested in is getting the name and address of the cute guy on the cover. The author of the book, Mr. Diment, writes back to her. The letter, probably written by a hired-hand writer, is full of typing and spelling errors.

In the fifth book in the series, *E, My Name Is Emily*, Bunny's best friend writes to another author, G. R. Immerman, about her or his book *Great Bones*. (Norma's use of initials rather than names is her way of suggesting that there is no single, named author writing these books.) Emily receives an even more surprising reply:

> "Dear Emily, There are some rules for writing, I suppose, but most of them aren't very helpful. My own rule is to know what I want to say, say it, and get the hell out. I don't like actors who hang around smirking at the

audience, waiting for applause. Since I'm not a teacher,
this may all be a crock and you can forget it. As for my
personal life, that's my business, not yours. Read my
books. That's all you need to know about me. G. R.
Immerman" (52)

Norma's frustration about the lack of quality books for young
adolescent readers, written by authors who have a passion for writing,
was the impetus for the five books of her best friends series. What one
Kirkus reviewer wrote about one of the books, *C, My Name Is Cal*,
could apply to them all: [This book] is ". . . deftly sketched . . .
Mazer's skill in telling the reader more about Cal than he knows
himself, while narrating in Cal's unique, taciturn voice, is especially
memorable."[10] As this reviewer and many others intimate, all five of
the alphabet, best friends books are far more than the formula fiction
that has become enormously popular with young readers. These five
novels are as carefully crafted as the rest of Norma's fiction is. They
have real stories with authentic characters who face real issues. They
are books with protagonists we can care about—characters who are
memorable. Their plots are intriguing, and as in all of Norma's
fiction, they can be divided by the number three. Each of the books has
a main plot that deals with family problems the protagonist is facing.
The major subplot is the friendship, fraught with conflict, between the
protagonist and her or his best friend. A minor subplot is the
developing relationships between the protagonist, the best friend, and
members of the opposite sex. In each book the protagonist is
embarrassed as she or he attempts to negotiate these rough waters.
Although there is a similar structure to each book, reading any one of
them is not like reading the others. And, unlike most series books,
they have received favorable reviews from serious critics.

Norma reports with chagrin and resignation that after the fifth
book, Scholastic decided to stop publishing the series. Although they
were selling well by her standards, they were not selling well enough
for the series book market. The books had achieved Norma's goals:
kids were reading them; critics liked them; they were real books
written with passion. Norma finds what happened disheartening, but
she is proud of the books and would not succumb to writing a new title
every month or allowing her name to be used on books written by a
stable of hired writers.

Other Works for Young Readers

Two additional works by Norma Fox Mazer for young adolescent readers are: *Supergirl* and "Tuesday of the Other June," which appeared in *Short Takes: A Short Story Collection for Young Readers* edited by Elizabeth Segel.

Supergirl (1984) is the only adaptation from a screenplay that Norma has written. She freely admits that she did it for money. The advance, she says, was at the time about as much as she was earning a year in royalties. When she was working on the project it was kept secret—she didn't even tell her family what she was doing. It is ironic that this woman who nearly threw away her son's comics because they were lurid, racist, and sexist, has written a novel based on a comic book heroine.

Part of what made Norma do it, in addition to the money, was the opportunity to write about a feminist Supergirl. She does this admirably. Supergirl, of the movie and the book, is Superman's cousin. Her name is Kara, and she comes to earth from the City of Argo, where her people had escaped before the destruction of Krypton. It is the power of Omegahedron that keeps Argo, a domed city, alive. When the power escapes because of Kara's carelessness, she commandeers a spaceship and sets off on a journey through the pathway between outer and inner space. Once on earth, she must find the Omegahedron. She takes on the body of a very realistic adolescent schoolgirl, Linda Lee. Linda Lee, through Norma's deft use of dialogue, becomes a likeable character with typical adolescent foibles and problems. However, unlike typical schoolgirls, she must unleash all of her powers to combat evil.

This, by Norma's standards, is a slight novel. It is fun; it is humorous. Most importantly, it has a "comic book" protagonist who is neither racist, sexist, nor excessively violent. Through realistic dialogue and third-person narration, Norma creates an authentic adolescent supergirl. The novel would be fun to read aloud to younger adolescents and to suggest to those girls who are comic book fanatics.

While *Supergirl* is a light-weight novel, "Tuesday of the Other June" is a short story for young adolescents or older children that packs a punch. In a few short pages, June's personality is carefully developed. We know her as the daughter of a mother who is raising her on her own—one of the working poor of Norma's childhood. May, her mother (her grandmother was April) tells June that she must always do well and always be good. To May, being anything but good will add to their already numerous troubles.

Of course, trouble is on the horizon in the name of the Other June. June meets the Other June at swimming class each Tuesday. At first she tries to befriend her, but soon learns the Other June is a bully. June, the daughter of May, walks away from the trouble, but she cannot hide from the Other June:

> And it seemed to me that this would go on forever, that Tuesdays would come forever and I would be forever trapped by the side of the pool, the Other June whispering *Buffalo Brain Fish Eyes Turkey Nose* into my ear, while she ground her elbow into my side and smiled her square smile at the swimming teacher. (9-10)

Finally, swimming class ends and June rejoices.

If this were a lesser author, this might be the end of the story. However, Norma's story will not end without an additional rising action and a denouement. June's mother has the opportunity to become the manager of a building, giving them free rent. June does not want to move, but has no choice. When they go to visit the new apartment, June sees the Other June across the street. She knows that the Other June will remain a part of her life. As with many of Norma's characters, she dreads starting in her new school. Her worst fears are realized—the Other June is in her class and says to her teacher, "She can sit next to me, Mr. Morrisey" (14). Now, everyday is Awfulday—every class is swimming class. The Other June follows June, daughter of May, around during recess, droning in her ear. "You are my slave, you must do everything I say, I am your master, say it, say, 'Yes, master, you are my master'" (14). June, granddaughter of April, presses her lips together, refusing to respond or be taunted. The next morning the Other June is waiting as she leaves the house. June dreams of "kicking her, punching, biting like a dog" (15). And, in spite of the virtue of her mother's advice, we wish she would.

One day the teacher leaves the classroom. As is typical, the kids begin to act out—one boy climbs on Mr. Morrisey's desk. The Other June stabs pencils into June, daughter of May, breaking her skin. June, granddaughter of April, has had enough. She flies to her feet screaming, "*Noooooo*" (16):

> The Other June's eyes opened, popped wide like the eyes
> of somebody in a cartoon. It made me laugh. The boy on
> the desk laughed, and then the other kids were laughing,
> too. (16)

She leans toward the Other June, poking her finger against her chest. Mr. Morrisey returns to the class and asks the two Junes what is going on. June jabs her finger into the Other June's chest, saying "No—more" (17):

> She turned around, staring at him with that big-eyed
> cartoon look. After a moment she sat down at her desk
> with a loud slapping sound.
>
> Even Mr. Morrisey laughed.
>
> And sitting at my desk, twirling my braids, I knew
> this was the last Tuesday of the Other June. (17)

June finds the chink in the Other June's armor—she cannot stand to be humiliated in front of her peers. The story, told in the authentic voice of a young adolescent, deals with a mature issue in a way young readers can understand and celebrate.

Notes

1. V. S. Pritchett, quoted in Norma Fox Mazer, "Growing Up with Stories," *Top of the News* (Winter 1985): 161.
2. Norma Fox Mazer, "Why I Write. . . . Why I Write What I Write," *The ALAN Review* (Spring 1987): 49.
3. Sally Holmes Holtz, *Presenting Norma Fox Mazer* (Twayne Publishers, 1987): 43.
4. Holtz, *Presenting Norma Fox Mazer,* 61.
5. Norma Fox Mazer, "Why I Write. . . . ," *Indirections* (September 1990): 13-14.
6. Mazer, "Why I Write. . . . ," 14.
7. Norma Fox Mazer, "Bread, Books, and Passion," *Signal* (1988-1989): 1.
8. Norma Fox Mazer, "Comics, Cokes, & Censorship," *Top of the News* (January 1976): 167.
9. Mazer, "Comics, Cokes, & Censorship," 167.
10. Review of *C, My Name Is Cal, Kirkus Review* (December 1, 1990): 1676.

Chapter 6

Fantasy and Suspense

"A good story," according to Norma Fox Mazer is the most important thing in fiction. To her that means "a story worth telling, a story with some weight, with conflict, contradiction, and struggle." The second most important element in fiction, according to Mazer, is "characters who are real and interesting people."[1] Throughout her life Mazer has sought out good stories. As a schoolgirl she didn't much enjoy her science classes because there weren't any stories. Today, she muses that this is too bad because there are lots of good stories in science. When she discovered anthropology as an academic discipline, she loved it—it was full of good stories. She read and reread Colin Turnball's *The Gentle People*, a book about pygmies of the Ituri Forest, and Laurens van der Post's treatise on the bushmen of the Kalihari.

Because story is so important to Mazer it comes as no surprise to discover that she has written novels in the genres of fantasy and suspense—both require a good story.

Mazer considers herself to be a writer who primarily explores domestic relationships. This is also true in her fantasy and suspense novels. In that way, they are as realistic as all her fiction. However, her objective in writing is not realism. It is story, and she will tell the story in whatever way it needs to be told.

Saturday, the Twelfth of October

Saturday, the Twelfth of October (1975) is Mazer's third novel and her only foray into the genre of fantasy. She wrote the novel because she was fascinated by stories of ancient peoples and she found herself wondering what it would be like to travel through time to an ancient culture. As with all of her fiction, she began by asking questions. One day, by chance, she happened upon a public television show on the Tassaday people, who were alleged to have lived on the Philippine Islands, as people had lived during the Stone Age, totally removed from modern civilization. Anthropologists looked at them as a living glimpse into prehistoric times. (Since that time, Mazer points out, we have learned that the Tassaday were, indeed, removed from modern culture, but they were far more advanced than anthropologists originally believed.) However, this show—these people—intrigued Mazer. She began to imagine a story of an ordinary girl from the twentieth century finding herself among Stone Age people.

Mazer still maintains that *Saturday* was one of the most difficult novels she has written—it took her several years to complete. It also remains one of her favorites. She began by researching—reading reports of anthropologists who had lived with tribal peoples. She wrote and rewrote, having her first ever anxiety attack, "sitting up in bed at night, gasping for air, wondering if I could carry out the story."[2] Her first manuscript was rejected by her editor Ron Buehl who called it an outline of a book. Finally, after much pain and hard work, she had an accepted, completed manuscript she sent out to readers and critics, knowing the story was now theirs to interpret—no longer hers alone. The most hurtful review on any of her books was a *New York Times Book Review* of *Saturday* by young-adult author Barbara Wersba that primarily praised the book but criticized its "biological realism."[3] However, the comment that most buoyed her was from an anthropologist who affirmed the book—that the culture was realistic, it was correct.

In the book Mazer creates a matriarchal society in which the menarche is honored and celebrated. The culture has its own language, customs, games, family structure, mores, and traditions. It also is a book of social criticism—comparing the ills of modern society to the simpler ways of the People.

The story revolves around Zan Ford, a completely modern fourteen-year-old girl, whose brother Ivan reads her very private diary to two of his friends. In her diary she has revealed her most personal thoughts, fears, and anxieties: the family's crowded living conditions (Zan sleeps on a cot in the kitchen), having been mugged, and worry about not having menstruated. Zan is more than angry at her brother—she is furious beyond words. She feels as if she has been mugged again. She flees her home, running to her favorite rock in Mechanix Park.

Here is where the time travel begins, and is probably the weakest part of the story. Mazer's strengths are in telling stories and revealing characters, not in moving us from place to place. Several reviewers agree with this assessment. Alethea K. Helbig and Agnes Regan Perkins write, "Zan's otherworld journey is never satisfactorily explained or integrated with her real life story."[4] Sally Holmes Holtz concurs that the time journeys are not as successful as the portrayal of another time.[5]

Throughout much of Zan's time with the People, she worries about her journey back home. It is almost as if her creator, Norma Fox Mazer, is worrying aloud with her. However, this small weakness is made up for in Mazer's vivid and anthropologically accurate description of the People and their culture.

Zan awakes, after her physically abusing journey, on a meadow covered with exotic vegetation. She is afraid—lost in an unfamiliar world. When she looks down at herself she realizes that she has not changed. Her clothing is still as it was, and she feels a sudden fondness for it. She fingers each of the objects in her pockets: her jackknife, a white button, a crumpled tissue, a safety pin, two linty lifesavers, her school locker key. She calls out.

Soon she sees a girl who has been watching her, and with her is a boy—Burrum—and her cousin Sonte. They call Zan "Meezzan" (from "Me Zan") and take her home to the People, the tribe of Stone Age cave dwellers to which they belong. Zan is, not surprisingly, terrified of these strange people with their strange ways and even stranger food.

So that her readers can learn more about the ways of the People, Mazer shifts the voice of the story from Zan's to Burrum's, as she looks forward to an annual festival, "the Sussuru for all the girls whose blood had come down for the first time." (42)

In a subsequent chapter, Sonte tells us about the culture of the People from the male perspective. In a chapter written in the voice of Diwera, the medicine woman, Mazer sets up the matriarchal society of the People. Although we have met strong female protagonists in Mazer's earlier novels (Trissy in *I, Trissy* and Jenny Pennoyer in *A Figure of Speech*), this is the first time we understand the author's perspective on the role of women in society. Mazer's female characters are not only strong, and to some degree dominant, they are the central figures in each family. In those novels in which there is no mother (*Downtown, Taking Terri Mueller,* and *When She Was Good*), something is wrong—the world is upset.

Saturday, the Twelfth of October can be examined as a feminist novel. Being female is honored and celebrated—the role of the birth-mother revered. Women are the leaders of the tribe. In the novel, Zan comes to learn that this reverence for women is missing from modern society, and she regrets that getting her period is considered unmentionable—that she was embarrassed when Ivan and his friends read about her concerns in her diary. The reviewers of *Saturday, the Twelfth of October* missed this important point when they complained that the novel dwelt too much on menstruation.

In a recent adult essay, "What's the Big Idea Anyway?," appearing in the book *Hot Flashes: Women Writers on the Change of Life,* edited by Lynne Taetsch, Mazer reflects on the importance of menstruation in contemporary society:

> When you have menstruated from the age of thirteen to the age of fifty-six, as I did, for forty-three years in other words, the end does not sneak up on you. When it's over, it's over. Gone is your monthly cycle, the miserable lows, the thrilling highs. Gone is the annoyance of inspecting your sheets and underpants to see if they're stained, of getting rid of bloody tampons and napkins. And gone too, is the way in which you count and note the passing of time. When you are menstruating, things happen "just before my period . . . while I was having my period . . . the month I missed my period and was petrified . . ." Gone too, is the possibility that you might produce life again.[6]

Diwera goes to Zan and through her actions convinces her that she will not survive if she does not learn the ways of the People. The story of Zan's first meeting with Diwera is told from Zan's perspective:

All at once the woman snatched a handful of hair from Zan's head, yanked it straight from her scalp.

"Uhhh!" Zan cried.

Rolling the hair in one hand, the woman turned and took a live ember from the fire. She dripped the ember into the nest of hair, which flared up, crackling, and burnt in her palm with a penetrating acrid odor. Spitting into her palm, she mixed the ashes and saliva with a forefinger. Still chanting, she rubbed the mixture of spit and ashes across Zan's forehead and down both cheeks. (83)

Mazer frequently uses fire symbolically to denote a passing—a life change. Remember the trash can fire that Trissy set in *I, Trissy* and the burning of Emily's half sister's photograph in *E, My Name Is Emily*.

For most young readers, this is where the real story begins. All of the previous had been descriptions of the culture and setting up the story. This is probably why this book was not as popular with adolescents as many of Mazer's books. Sophisticated readers can appreciate the skill with which she has established the Stone Age, matriarchal society, but most young readers can't.

Zan never loses her desire to go home, but more and more she enjoys life with Burrum and Sonte. She comes to love the forest and enjoy the games of the young people. She is accepted into Burrum's large family. However, Diwera, although fascinated by and attracted to Zan, also fears her strange ways and power, symbolized by her possessions. Zan, too, is afraid of Diwera, recognizing her healing power, suspicion, and influence.

Zan now dresses like the People, but she still clings to her few possessions, particularly those that were in her pockets. She shows them to the other children, but will not allow them to touch. The children call them: *Nii'uff*, *Kee*, *Baa'tun*, and *Saf'tee Pan*. Burrum's blood comes and she, without Meezzan, will participate in the Sussuru. Zan is happy for her, but feels the outsider—watching the events of the week-long coming-of-age ceremony. She also knows that after the ceremony, Burrum will no longer run with children as she had done before.

Zan is with the People for almost a year. During this time, Zan and the readers learn of the birthing rituals of the People when Yano delivers her baby at the birthing spot she has prepared near the river. As time goes on, Diwera becomes increasingly concerned about

Meezzan, her strange ways, and her "powerful" possessions. The climax comes when Hiffaru, Diwera's son, steels Nii'uff. He is jealous of Sonte because he is handsome and Hiffaru's face is deformed. They fight, and Hiffaru fatally wounds Sonte with the knife—the first murder in the memory of the People. In the pandemonium following the murder, Zan flees, feeling guilty about what has happened and terrified for her own life. Without knowing how, she is transported home.

The ending of the novel is less satisfactory than the time Zan spends with the people, however by modern standards it is probably realistic. Zan, thinking she has been gone for a year, comes home to find nothing changed—no one has missed her. She learns from her mother that it is still the same day—Saturday, the twelfth of October. When she attempts to tell them of the People, they send her to a psychiatrist. However, her journey has helped her become more at peace with herself and with her life. We are not sure whether the journey actually happened. We are left in suspense—"Mazer never lets readers know for sure whether Zan's experience is real or schizophrenic escape"[7]—but we do know that Zan has changed. She has grown up, her period has begun, and she will never be the same. Mazer implies that this is the journey of all women, not only those with an otherworld experience.

Taking Terri Mueller

Many of Mazer's books grow from a single sentence that appears, almost magically, in her head. *Taking Terri Mueller* came to her in this way. Mazer says that once she had the sentence—"a girl is kidnapped by her father"—the hard work was over. Now all she had to do was ask a myriad of questions about that sentence. Questions such as: Why? How? When?[8] That does not mean that writing the novel was easy. In Mazer's world, there is nothing more important than motherhood. Taking a child away from her mother is unimaginable; and when that child is kidnapped by her father, it is unforgivable. This posed a dilemma for Mazer. How could she paint a sympathetic picture of a father who had stolen his daughter away from her mother?

Mazer had an image of her character Phil in her mind. "He was a great dad, relaxed, loving, and attentive, but I hated him for kidnapping his daughter, and the emotion put me in a writer's gridlock."[9] She broke through the block unexpectedly. One day she came upon a picture in a magazine of a man holding a baby up toward his face, smiling at the baby with ecstatic love. The picture helped her understand Phil's motivation for kidnapping Terri. Mazer tore the picture out of the magazine and hung it over her typewriter. Everyday, before she did anything else, she looked at the picture and thought, "This is the way Terri's father feels about her. This was how much he loved her as an infant and has gone on loving her."[10] Finally, Mazer could write the novel because she could comprehend what losing Terri would mean to Phil.

However, we do not know about the kidnapping until well into the novel. That scene occurs about halfway through, and by the time we get there, we have come to know Phil, appreciate his relationship with Terri, and understand his painful need to keep her ignorant of the truth.

The novel starts with an almost perfect father-daughter relationship. Terri is thirteen, strong and independent:

> She was a tall girl with long hair that she sometimes wore
> in a single braid down her back . . . She was quiet and
> watchful and didn't talk a lot, although she liked to talk,
> especially to her father, with whom she felt she could talk
> about anything. (12)

In the above description of Terri, we see one of the techniques Mazer frequently uses—what she calls, the rhythm of three:[11] (1) "a tall girl"; (2) "with long hair...in a single braid down her back"; (3) "quiet...didn't talk a lot, although she liked to talk." We notice the same technique in a brief description of the apparently mature, equal relationship between Terri and her father:

> They didn't have too many rules in their life because Phil
> said—and Terri agreed—that the main rule was to be
> thoughtful about each other. That covered a lot of territory,
> such as each of them letting the other know where they
> were at all times, and not waiting for the other person to
> clean up any messes Barkley [the dog] made. In the car,
> though, they did have rules, such as no eating peanuts in
> the shell (too messy), and no soft drinks (Phil didn't
> approve of caffeine), and no driving while sleeping. That
> was Terri's rule for Phil, because she wasn't old enough
> yet to share the driving. (11)

We are beginning to learn that there are some unusual things in
their lives together. For example, they never stay in one place very
long. Phil says this is because of his "itchy feet." However, we wonder.
Phil seems too intelligent to be working as a handyman. Terri tells us
that they have lived in so many different apartments that she thinks of
their Pinto as their home. She is beginning to wonder why her father
insists on being carried through life by his "instincts," as he tells her.
Why can't they have a home—stay in one place so that she can make
some friends?

The novel begins in a new apartment in a new town, this time
Ann Arbor, Michigan. Terri is in a new school and makes a new
friend, Shaundra, a classmate from a divorced family. Phil begins a
relationship with a young divorcée, Nancy Briet, who has a son, Lief,
who is about the age Terri was when her mother was killed in a car
accident—or, at least, that's what Phil tells her. Terri wonders why he
won't talk about her mother more, why there are no pictures of her.

Once a year Terri's Aunt Vivian, Phil's spinster sister, comes to
visit. One day she chances upon a photograph in Aunt Vivian's wallet
of her with a man and two boys. But Aunt Vivian is single—who are
these people? She begins to ask Vivian lots of questions, not about the
picture, but about her mother and the accident that killed her. That
night she overhears Vivian and Phil talking and knows they have a
secret that involves her.

She and her friend Shaundra break into a locked box that belongs
to Phil. In the box she finds a certificate of divorce for her parents,
dated a year after her mother was supposedly killed. Now she must
confront her father—she has to know the secret, the lie. She does so in
front of Nancy, forcing him to admit he has lied.

Mazer uses an interesting technique to emphasize the importance
of the scene in which Terri confronts her father. The entire confrontation is revealed through Terri's thoughts as she is recalling the
events of the previous weekend while sitting in a class in school. The
scene is printed in italics in the text:

> *I don't want to tell you, he said. I don't want to tell you.*
> *It's up to you, Terri. It's up to Terri. We can stop this*
> *right now. We can just forget it . . . go back to the way*
> *things were . . . (88)*

But he and Terri both know there is no going back. He has told Terri that Kathryn, her mother, did not die, that Kathryn had told him after the custody battle that she was remarrying and moving to Italy. He told Terri that he had planned what he was going to do, and the next visiting day he was ready. They drove all night. Terri was good, he'd given her half a tranquilizer to be sure. He told her stories, and they sang as they drove. At first she cried a lot at night, but he would hold her. Suddenly, in the midst of her father's admission, Nancy cries out in shock: *"What you're saying, Phil . . . You're saying you kidnapped her. You kidnapped your own daughter. My god, Phil, my god"* (95). Terri can't get the word out of her mind. It makes no sense to her, how could her father be a kidnapper?

The second half of the novel deals with the search. Terri soon understands that knowing her mother is alive is not enough—she must find her, see her.

She first tries to call her mother in Oakland, California, but can find no listing. She tells her father she has been calling Oakland and begs him to give her Aunt Viv's address so she can write to her and see if she knows her mother's whereabouts. Aunt Viv tells Terri of her own moral dilemma in keeping Phil's secret and now in giving Terri her mother's address and phone number. Aunt Viv admits to Terri that one of her greatest fears has been, and continues to be, that Phil will be arrested. Aunt Viv confides in Terri that she is afraid of what Kathryn might do if she finds out, and although torn, gives Terri Kathryn's name, address, and phone number because she believes it is the right thing to do. Terri must weigh the risks and do what she thinks is best, placing the moral dilemma in the hands of a thirteen-year-old. This dilemma is the second level of the issue addressed in the novel—will the truth hurt more by knowing it?

Terri, too, is terrified of calling her mother. But she must speak to her; knowing she is alive is not enough. Shaundra, who learned of the divorce decree with Terri, violates the confidence by telling George, a boy in their class in whom Terri is interested. Terri is furious. This is another issue addressed in the novel: Whom can we trust and how far should we trust them?

On another level, this novel, like *Downtown* and *Missing Pieces*, is about secrets and lies and what they do to relationships. Mazer frequently deals with this issue in her writing. In *Taking Terri Mueller* the lie has affected numerous relationships: Terri and her mother and, of course, Terri and her father; Phil and Vivian; Terri and Vivian;

Terri, Phil, and Vivian's family; Vivian and her family; Phil and Nancy. And, throughout Terri's life and Phil's life with her, every other relationship they have ever had has been affected by this lie. In this novel, Mazer again shows, as critic Sally Holmes Holtz suggests, that "the truth . . . is preferable to euphemisms and lies."[12]

When Terri makes the call, her mother is not sure whether to believe it is her daughter, even when Terri can answer questions she might not otherwise know. Terri calls again and learns that she has a little sister, Leah. Her mother is beginning to believe that it is really Terri, and she begs her to come visit. Terri has not told Kathryn where she is, and she limits her conversations so the phone calls cannot be traced. Her mother tells her that she is willing to consider the past, past. All she wants to do is see Terri. Nancy convinces Phil to call Kathryn and arrange for Terri to go to California for Christmas. At first he resists, but he does it. Terri is going to see her mother.

On the plane we learn her thoughts through a letter to her father and a diary entry she writes. Her arrival in California is over-whelming—she is greeted by her mother and a large crowd of neighbors, family, and other well-wishers. After the initial shock wears off, she begins to enjoy life with her California family.

Mazer changes voices. Kathryn, the first morning Terri is in her home, tells us of the intervening years. We learn of all the questions she has about Terri and about her life—the life she has missed. She remembers the years of searching, of hiring detectives, running newspaper ads and stories—all worthless.

At first Leah is jealous of Terri, but this passes. Terri enjoys being a part of a larger family and loves all of the attention she is getting. She now must decide if she will stay with Kathryn and her new family or return to Phil. She gets a letter from Nancy telling her that she is breaking off with Phil because he will not admit that kidnapping Terri was wrong. Ironically, it is this letter that causes her to reconsider the decision she has made to stay in California. She loves Phil, and although she cannot accept what he has done, she decides to return to her father, planning to spend part of every year with her mother.

This is a well-crafted novel, using the literary techniques Mazer has perfected in earlier stories. Critics commend it for being "well-written, fast-paced . . ." reaching "amazing emotional depths . . ."[13] Critic Dick Abrahamson writes that Mazer "does a fine job of taking Terri through the emotional ups and downs caused by her discovery."[14] Terri is a remarkable protagonist. "We believe in just about everything Terri does, because [Mazer's] writing makes us willing to believe. She wins us completely with this finely wrought and moving book."[15]

Her ability to examine an issue without being judgmental is also recognized. She "has looked at the issue from all angles and successfully conveys the overwhelming emotional impact inherent in the situation."[16] Her characters are well developed and strong. "All . . . are very human. Both parents are portrayed sympathetically."[17]

Taking Terri Mueller, as reviewer Dick Abrahamson suggests, is "One of Mazer's best." In it we see not only her ability to craft a novel, but her art of making a difficult issue the spine of a novel and bringing it to life through the creation of believable and sympathetic characters—some of whom we find ourselves liking when our reason tells us we should hate them. This emotional story, written on many levels with unusual depth for a young adult suspense novel, deals with important ethical dilemmas which are worth considering. Recipient of the Edgar Allan Poe Award for a juvenile mystery, it ends with hope— perhaps the one gift Mazer wants to give her readers. According to critic Sally Holmes Holtz, the message of the novel is "inspirational, but not didactic; it is a thought-provoking view presented through the lives of [the] characters . . . "[18]

Out of Control

Mazer's second suspense novel *Out of Control* (1993) was written more than a decade after *Taking Terri Mueller*. Although the books are quite different, they also have many similarities. *Out of Control*, like her earlier suspense novel, began with a single sentence—actually a phrase: "Thirty seconds that changed the world." Several years earlier, after Mazer had been a guest speaker at a school, the librarian drove her to her motel. On the way, she told Mazer of an "incident" that had occurred that day. Two boys had grabbed a girl, pulled her into a corner, and molested her. The librarian told Mazer about the hornet's nest this incident had created. "What a mess," the librarian said. "And you know, the whole thing happened in thirty seconds."[19] That was all Mazer needed; she had the phrase that would serve as the spine for a new book:

Astonishing. My heart beat hard. I was like a dog
with a bone, afraid it would be taken from me. I scribbled
words on a piece of paper. When I looked at it five
minutes later, it was indecipherable. No matter. I could no
sooner have forgotten what she had said than I could have
forgotten the names of my children. But still, taking no
chances, I wrote it down, only it came out this way:
"Thirty seconds that changed the world."

Then I scribbled a few phrases: "30 seconds . . . it all
happened in thirty seconds, less than a minute . . . the
random and chaotic nature of life . . . the confluence of
events and personalities . . . like raging streams that pour
together at some point and swell into a flood . . . do one
small thing, everything changes . . ." [20]

As with *Taking Terri Mueller* there is a clear unity of opposites in
Out of Control: three boys and one unusual girl. And before she wrote
the first word of the novel, there is a scene that Mazer knew had to be
written—the thirty seconds of the molestation of that girl by those
boys. Now she had to give her story lifeblood—she had to create
characters we could believe in and come to like. This was a difficult
task, nearly as difficult as turning Phil into a likeable kidnapper in
Taking Terri Mueller.

However, there was another event, another person whose story
needed to be told. Perhaps she could appear in this book. Several years
earlier Mazer had been in a bookstore in Philadelphia when a young
retarded woman came up to her with the glowing face of a child. She
told Mazer excitedly that it was her birthday—that she was thirty-three
and her Mommy had given her money to buy a Nancy Drew book.
Mazer, smiling, wished her happy birthday. The young woman threw
her arms around Mazer, gave her a kiss, telling her, "You are my
favorite person! You are a lovely, lovely person!"[21] Mazer knew, at
that moment, that she had to tell her story.

So, these two disparate events, "the random chaotic nature of
life," joined together to form *Out of Control*. The first chapter
introduces us to the three boys. They are popular, intelligent, and
athletic. Rollo is on the football team, Candy is president of the
student senate, and Brig is a star pitcher and president of the Honor
Society. They have been good friends for a long time—maybe too
long. They are interested in girls, but only certain girls. They are
egocentric and can be mocking and cruel. "They all watch a tall girl

crossing the street. She's wearing a long coat, men's work boots, and a gray fedora with a big droopy feather in the brim" (14). When this girl attempts to walk up the steps to the school, they block her access, and she steps on Brig's hand. Unlike the boys, she is strong and independent. Each of the boys is a follower, easily swayed by the others. Ilene Cooper says of the boys and their friendship, "What [Mazer] gets very right is the importance to Rollo of being one with his friends—how good that feels, better than feeling honorable."[22]

However when Rollo is home, a different personality emerges. His mother died when he was a young boy. His older sister, Kara, is retarded and we learn later that she has Down's syndrome. What surprises us—changes our opinion of Rollo—is his treatment of Kara. He treats her without condescension and tells her stories and jokes, even though she doesn't understand. Rollo truly seems to like her: rather than feel embarrassed by her or ashamed of her handicap, he is proud of her accomplishments, her work at McDonald's.

But then he is back in school with Brig and Candy and caught up in their shenanigans. They are in the cafeteria playing a game. They pick a girl, stare her down, and then bet on what she is going to do. Often they are correct. On this particular day, they stare down Valerie Michon, the girl who stepped on Brig's hand. When she realizes they are staring at her, she stares back. "The game's no fun with her. They should have known" (27).

Valerie is a serious girl—an honors student and an artist—but even though she is strong, she lacks self-confidence. She is a girl who exudes confidence and strength, but is actually an outsider who feels left out and lonely. Her appearance and the clothes she wears separate her even more from her peers. But she looks at her dress as an expression of her artistry.

Brig has a girlfriend, Arica, who is trying to break up with him. One day Arica, Rollo, and Brig go to McDonald's after school. Rollo, trying to avoid Arica flirting with him, calls Kara over to the table. When he introduces her to Arica, it is clear she is uncomfortable meeting her. Kara tells her, "Arica, I love you!" (40). She kisses Arica's cheek and neck. Later Arica says to Rollo, after he's told her about Kara's Down's syndrome, "I thought it was something like that. Is she always that goofy?" (41). Rollo doesn't put Arica down, but he makes it clear that Kara is not goofy. We like him for how he handles both his sister and Brig's girlfriend.

A day or two later when the boys are together they see Valerie in the hall at school. Brig veers toward her and she gets a look of terror on her face which the boys find hilarious. "They go straight for her, rushing, like a mini-phalanx, like war. At the last moment, Brig puts out his hands as if he's going to grab her tits. And then, at the last last moment, he veers off, and they sweep by her" (43). That night Valerie calls Brig and tells him to keep away from her. The confrontations are getting nastier.

On the way toward the final confrontation, Mazer develops a subplot which serves as an interesting counterpoint to the main plot. Valerie is tutoring Mark Saddler, a boy from a working class home in the town of Union. He is very different from the popular protagonist and his friends. Mark is poor, works many hours each day, and has difficulty with his school work.

One day, when Brig is reeling after an argument with Arica, he takes his parents' car without their knowledge and convinces Rollo to drive with him to Union. On the way, traveling very fast over snow-covered roads, they come within feet of hitting a deer. They respond with enthusiastic excitement. They laugh and keep laughing as they push the car out of a snow bank—not concerned about the car, their safety, or killing the deer. In Union they look for Mark's house, calling him Grutty—their term for people who live in Union. When they find the house, Mark is coming out on his way to work. They tell him he'd better watch out for his girlfriend. "Valerie Michon. She's unnatural . . . You know the type, she's like a guy in disguise" (68). They are excited, barely breathing—loving this confrontation. Mark tells them to get out. They sit in their cars waiting for the other to go first. Brig pulls away, skidding his car close to Saddler's as he passes.

The morning of the molestation there is a Christmas assembly in school. The boys sit together and see Valerie walk out. They leave, following her. Mazer's description of the molestation is purposefully vague, but at the same time we know exactly what happens:

> And then they all grab her. They just do it, all together. It happens fast, so fast. It's like reading each other's minds. *Let's get her.* Did Brig say that? They don't say anything now, they just grab her, and you can't tell who does what, whose hands are where.
>
> "Stop! Quit! Oh, damn, no . . . oh . . . oh . . . stop. . ."
>
> Rollo hears panting. Maybe it's himself. He hears and grunts, and he's aware of his hot breath. His face and

hands are burning, and his hands are on Valerie: he has
some part of her in his hand, some soft flesh, some
thrilling part of her. (86)

This is the thirty seconds that changes the world for all of them.
They return to the auditorium, but are soon called to the principal's
office. Mr. Ferranto confronts them with what Valerie has told him.
They stick to their story, saying it is a bunch of lies, only admitting
that they were on the third floor and that they did shove her. Mr.
Ferranto tells them, "Do you understand that your whole life might be
changed by your mean and thoughtless actions?" (100). He sends them
home, telling them not to talk to anyone about this.

In a letter to the superintendent we learn why Mr. Ferranto
doesn't want them to talk about the incident:

> As I see it, we face two problems. (1) To ascertain the
> truth from the conflicting stories of the three boys and the
> girl. (2) Damage control.
> To be blunt, Sam, the second problem is the one that
> concerns me most . . . (104)

Mr. Ferranto is in many ways the villain—perhaps more so than
the boys. However, reviewer Carolyn Noah in *School Library Journal*
writes, "The efforts of the school to contain possible negative publicity,
even at Valerie's expense, are painful and have the ring of truth."[23]

The principal sees his dilemma as whether his duty to keep calm
in the school outweighs his responsibility to Valerie. He takes the easy
way out—his duty to the school wins. He avoids confrontation with the
students, their parents, legal authorities, and the press.

The boys agree that they will stick to their story: things just got a
little out of hand. What Valerie has said is a bunch of lies. But Rollo is
beginning to crack—did nothing happen? By the next day, it is clear
that everyone knows. Some of the kids are treating them like heroes,
but with the girls it's different.

Valerie is terrified—she can't tell anyone what has happened, not
even her father. Her father had taught her that the world is good, and
she believed him. Now her beliefs are crumbling. When she meets
with Mr. Ferranto he is totally insensitive to her feelings. He tells her
that he and his wife, a psychologist, have discussed the incident, and
in order for her to begin healing the boys need to apologize to her. He
calls the boys into his office. In front of this terrified girl, he forces

them to apologize to her. Of course, the apology is a joke to the boys. When he asks Valerie if she accepts the apologies of the boys, she responds in the only way she can. "'Fuck you all,'" she says and walks out (129).

Over the winter holidays, Rollo begins to question what they did. He's still denying to himself his culpability, calling the incident "a minute of craziness, stupidity, foolishness—maybe not even a minute, maybe thirty seconds . . ." (131). He decides the adults are over-reacting.

Throughout the winter break, Rollo comes closer and closer to understanding the "rotten and vicious" thing he did (146). He is beginning to understand that friendship, when it leads to group mentality, can be dangerous.

Valerie's holidays are difficult—the incident stays with her, haunts her. She realizes the attack has changed her: before, she had positive feelings—she felt "brave and alert" (153), but now all she has is negative, hateful feelings. She hates the boys for what they have done; she despises the principal and how he has treated her. Afraid of everyone and everything, she sees little hope for her life.

However, for Rollo something begins to change. For some reason, he's not quite sure why, he wants to talk with her. We realize what Rollo doesn't, that he wants to talk to Valerie to free himself from his pain—to really apologize so that he can begin healing. What he does not understand is that an apology is not enough. His actions were too hurtful, too damaging. However, Rollo's persistence is beginning to affect Valerie.

Valerie is facing her own ethical dilemma. Can she forgive? Even though they have stolen something from her—something that we know is her innocence—is she willing to forgive? She begins to feel sympathy for Rollo and agrees to meet with him. But when they do he can't answer her questions: Why did you do this? What if someone did it to you? Even though the meeting changes nothing, both Rollo and Valerie are beginning the healing process.

One night Rollo takes Kara to a party. Suddenly Kara is gone—Rollo can't find her anywhere. He panics. He sees Valerie going into the ladies room and asks her to check if Kara is there. Finally, he finds his sister outside in the snow. She begs him to dance, but he tells her she's danced enough. Valerie says, almost to herself but aloud, "How can anyone dance *enough*?" (187). Kara and Valerie dance in the snow, laughing as they jump around. Valerie, who responds to Kara in much the way Rollo does, finds the beginning of her healing process in their dance. She can still laugh. This does not mean that her pain is over—she must still face her fear.

Rollo, too, is beginning to heal. He and the other two boys are suspended for two weeks following the holidays. His father helps him move toward health by suggesting that he needs to do something for someone other than himself. He takes the advice, going to the Senior Center each day of his two-week suspension. Rollo and his father begin to talk again, and when Rollo sees Brig and Candy he realizes that he does not want to tell them about his meetings with Valerie—he has nothing to say to them.

When the boys return to school, Mr. Ferranto calls Valerie into his office. He suggests to her that she might want to study at home or transfer to another school. Valerie realizes that he doesn't want *bad* publicity for the school. That weekend she writes a letter to the editor about the incident, planning to send it to the local paper or TV station. This positive, assertive act helps her heal more quickly.

By the end of this remarkably intense novel, all the major characters have changed, grown. We know that the incident will never leave them—they will never forget. However, they have begun to put it in perspective and live their lives.

In spite of a few weaknesses, this novel is one of Mazer's most interesting and readable works. Reviewers and young readers agree. Deborah Stevenson in the *Bulletin of the Center for Children's Books* says of the novel, Mazer "has worked this ethics-charged subject matter into a tight and readable novel, whose explorations of groupthink versus individual responsibility are reminiscent of *Killing Mr. Griffin* [by Lois Duncan]. This is gripping enough to deliver the recreational read the title and cover promise, but it could also prompt some extremely lively classroom discussion."[24]

Mazer's suspense novels are intriguing. They do not neatly fit into the genre because they are not written as either suspense or mystery. Instead, they are wonderful character studies that explore important issues.

Notes

1.   Norma Fox Mazer, "A Conversation with Norma Fox Mazer," *Writing!* (March 1985): 19.
2.   Adele Sarkissian, ed. *Something About the Author Autobiography Series,* Vol. 1. (Gale Research Company, 1986): 199.

3. Barbara Wersba, review of *Saturday, the Twelfth of October, The New York Times Book Review* (October 19, 1975): 12.

4. Alethea K. Helbig and Agnes Regan Perkins, eds. *Dictionary of American Children's Fiction, 1960-1984* (Greenwood Press, 1986): 575.

5. Sally Holmes Holtz, *Presenting Norma Fox Mazer* (Twayne Publishers, 1987): 25-29.

6. Norma Fox Mazer, "What's the Big Idea Anyway?," in *Hot Flashes: Woman Writers on the Change of Life*, Lynne Taetsch, ed. (Faber and Faber, 1995): 53.

7. Jack Forman, review of *Saturday, the Twelfth of October, School Library Journal* (November 1975): 93.

8. Norma Fox Mazer, "Breathing Life into a Story," *The ALAN Review* (September 1995): 13.

9. Mazer, "Breathing," 15.

10. Mazer, "Breathing," 15.

11. Norma Fox Mazer, "When You Write for Young Adults," *The Writer* (February 1986): 16.

12. Holtz, *Presenting*, 71.

13. Ilene Cooper, review of *Taking Terri Mueller, ALA Booklist*, (December 1, 1981): 500.

14. Dick Abrahamson, review of *Taking Terri Mueller, The ALAN Review* (Spring 1982): 15.

15. Review of *Taking Terri Mueller*, in *Contemporary Authors*, Vol. 32. James G. Lesniak, ed. (Gale Research Company, 1991): 290.

16. Review of *Taking Terri Mueller*, in *Kliatt Young Adult Paperback Book Guide* (January 1982): 13.

17. Karen Ritter, review of *Taking Terri Mueller, School Library Journal* (December 1981): 67.

18. Holtz, *Presenting*, 59.

19. Norma Fox Mazer, "Thirty Seconds, Eight Drafts, Three Years—and Then a Book," *The Writer* (December 1993): 19.

20. Mazer, "Thirty Seconds," 20.

21. Mazer, "Thirty Seconds," 20.

22. Ilene Cooper, review of *Out of Control, The New York Times Book Review* (May 16, 1993): 29.

23. Carolyn Noah, review of *Out of Control, School Library Journal* (March 1993): 222.

24. Deborah Stevenson, review of *Out of Control, Bulletin of the Center for Children's Books* (April 1993): 259.

Chapter 7

From Excellence to Mastery

"Perhaps I'm still looking for a story that will make it all clear,"[1] says Norma Fox Mazer. In March 1998 I asked Norma if she was still searching. "Yes," she chuckled, "I guess I am." She explained that her search is a quest to make sense out of life. Mazer is not religious—she describes herself as an atheist. She says if she believed in God, she could explain life, but because she does not, she must seek other explanations.

In three of Mazer's best works of fiction, spanning twenty-four years, we are privy to her search. In *Figure of Speech* (1973), *After the Rain* (1987), and *When She Was Good* (1997), Mazer examines life and death, love and abuse, and, most of all, the unity of family. To Mazer, families provide the strongest unity of life. It is in family that we find ourselves—our own identity. When this unity is broken, as it is in most of her novels, we lose not only our families, but often ourselves as well.

Perhaps this is why, as Harry told Norma when he read the first draft of *When She Was Good*, "It is too grim. There is no hope." Norma, as she frequently does when Harry gives her such an opinion, went into a rage, but when she cooled down she realized he was right. This is a book about a fractured family—a family beyond repair. To Mazer, when the family is gone, life loses its meaning. She rewrote the book, still her darkest story, giving Em, the book's protagonist, a sense of a future. Although she no longer has her biological family, there is hope in the book that she will again find herself through the unity of friendship and companionship—things she never had with her abusive family. Perhaps in this story Mazer is beginning to find her own meaning of life.

In spite of the darkness of *When She Was Good*, Mazer sees the world as basically good. Her characters are strong—they are survivors. This is particularly true of the young women in her novels. She observes life through the lenses of a feminist—not in a political or radical sense, but as a mother, a wife, a daughter, and now a grandmother, a member of a unified, multigenerational, largely female family. This unity of family, which when broken can destroy an individual, is the truth she explores in each of her novels.

A Figure of Speech

In *A Figure of Speech*, Mazer's second novel, we see evidence of her excellence as a crafter of stories and of fully developed protagonists. *A Figure of Speech* was honored as a finalist for the National Book Award. It has as its spine an issue that Mazer explores in numerous later novels and short stories—the story of a child's love for her grandfather and what happens when her family determines they can no longer care for him in their home. At its heart, it is about what happens within families when they begin to erode.

In the novel Mazer examines the problem of euphemisms—lies. Jenny Pennoyer, the young protagonist, recognizes that her family is not being honest with Grandpa. When they talk about him or within his hearing they speak in euphemisms. It seems to Jenny that because her grandfather is old, he is no longer treated like a person, no longer a part of their family. The real conflict between Jenny and her parents is over whether or not Grandpa should go to live in a nursing home. When the family visits Castle Haven, the nursing home they are considering for Grandpa Carl, Mrs. McCarthy, the manager, uses euphemisms to tell them:

> "Everyone in our Family has a complete health and personality file. We number code all our special diets.

> The chairs in the living room are numbered, so each
> resident has his own chair. It makes them feel more secure
> and cuts down on the bickering. I don't like bickering
> among my old people. I like them to be serene and happy
> in their twilight years. We like to think of this as a happy,
> happy place." (103)

Eventually, Jenny runs from the home, feeling helpless. She
knows there is nothing she can do. Her parents will bring Grandpa
Carl here, telling him they just want to see how he likes it, but what
they really will be doing is pushing him out of their home—just as
they pushed him out of his apartment in the basement.

Jenny was born thirteen years ago, the year Grandpa Carl moved
in with the family. Carl, who is eighty-three when the book begins, has
his own tiny apartment in the basement of the Pennoyer home where
Jenny goes to visit him every day, playing cards and listening to stories
about the old days. She sees Grandpa as warm and loving, but her
family are aggravated by the annoying notes he leaves on the family
bulletin board, like the one on the brown paper bag after his argument
with Jenny's mother, Amelia, about passing away. In his unmistakably
shaky hand he wrote in pencil on the bag:

> "I ain't going to 'pass away.' I'm going to die.
> "My time ain't going 'to come.' I'll be dead.
> "I ain't a 'senior citizen.' I'm an old codger of eighty
> three." (74)

Reviewer Karel Rose writes of *A Figure of Speech*, "the language
interchanges in the book are exciting. The old man always fights for
what is real in language and life, rejecting the euphemisms applied to
him."[2]

The Pennoyer home is small. One day, in an incident that seems a
bit contrived, older brother Vince tells his family he has dropped out
of college and he and his new wife, Valerie, are coming home to live.
Now the family is impossibly crowded and tensions begin to build.

In the aftermath of a cooking fire Grandpa has caused, Vince and
Valerie begin to repair the damage done downstairs. Grandpa is left
out of the work brigade. He becomes ill and spends ten days in bed.
When Jenny finally goes down to see the basement apartment, it has
been transformed into a brighter and cleaner space. Somehow she

begins to sense that Valerie and Vince are not doing all this work so that Grandpa can move back downstairs—they are doing it so they can have the apartment. The next day Jenny finds her mother sorting through Grandpa's clothes, putting his things in boxes to throw or give away. Jenny is appalled by her mother's lack of empathy. Although Grandpa does not know what is going on downstairs, his health is not improving and he seems to sense that he is being moved out of his home of thirteen years. As reviewer Hildegarde Gray writes of *A Figure of Speech,* Mazer's "painful, but proven . . ." point is "driven home with tremendous force . . . when we feel we are no longer needed, we begin to atrophy, physically and emotionally."[3]

The primary flaw in this novel, not evident in most of Mazer's later works, is the flatness of several of the family members. The lack of sensitivity of Amelia to her father-in-law's feelings seems contrived to make a point about the mistreatment and dehumanization of the elderly. Frank Pennoyer stands in the background allowing his wife Amelia to make the decisions about what will happen to his father. In later works, such as *Taking Terri Mueller* and *Out of Control,* her characters are far too well developed for us to dislike them so intensely. Here it appears the entire family is conspiring against Carl, attempting to move him out of the house—not because he is incapable of living there and largely taking care of himself, but because they are tired of him, want to be rid of him, and want the home for themselves. Intellectually, we can understand how Jenny's parents might feel, however we are never presented with their side of the story. Because they are undeveloped we cannot sympathize with their plight of living in a too small home with too little money and too many family members. We know nothing of what Amelia Pennoyer has endured during the thirteen years her father-in-law has lived in her home. Although Carl Pennoyer is, as he calls himself, "an old codger" who can be difficult, we know him as a more complete human being. Through his relationship with Jenny we see him as loving, intelligent, and kind. However, we only see Jenny's parents as cruel and uncaring. In a later novel about the Pennoyer family, *When We First Met,* we have the opportunity to get to know Jenny's parents, and they are far more complete and sympathetic characters. As reviewer and young-adult author Jill Paton Walsh states, "*A Figure of Speech* [is] . . . infused with a deeply felt compassion and humanity. And yet [it does not quite rise] . . . to the importance of the subject."[4]

Throughout most of the book we see Carl only through the eyes of Jenny, but in three chapters Mazer changes point of view and lets us see Carl through his own thoughts. In the first of these chapters, Jenny tells him that the family plans to take him to the nursing home to see if he likes it. She warns him that they will leave him there. That night Carl begins to plot his escape—he will go to his childhood farm, but first he will build his strength. He begins to take walks each day, and Amelia uses this as another defense for what they are about to do. She worries that he might get killed crossing the street. Jenny intuits Grandpa's motive for walking—she realizes that he plans to leave without her. She can't and won't let that happen. She runs after him and follows him onto a bus. Although he keeps telling her to go home, when they come to the end of the bus line he allows her to get on another bus with him. He, too, doesn't want to let go of his relationship with Jenny. He needs her as much or more than she needs him. Grandpa decides that he will let her come along for a few days and then will send her home, or maybe, he thinks, Frank will allow her to live with him. He feels betrayed by his son, but decides not to get upset about him anymore. "There wasn't going to be any Home for him. No home but his own home" (128). When they arrive at New Sayre, their destination country town, Jenny and Grandpa begin to walk the eight miles toward the family farm he remembers from when he was boy and a young man. Before they reach the deserted, run-down Pennoyer farm, Grandpa is breathing hard, sweating, and shaking. We recognize that they will not be able to survive on their own for long. The farmhouse is in much worse shape than either of them imagined—not a window is intact; the front door is hanging from a single hinge. Grandpa is grief stricken, but Jenny, in spite of her fear, remains optimistic. She begins to clean up the room that seems to be the least torn apart. However, the more she works, the more she realizes how impossible their task is. They have no firewood, no water, and the steps to the cistern have been vandalized. Even the old outhouse is unusable.

For a few days they are able to survive on apples and each other's warmth. However, one morning after a storm, Grandpa is not in bed. Jenny finds him, dead of exposure, under the old apple tree that has sustained them. In a sad and moving scene, she tries to bury him, but can dig only a shallow hole. She goes to the field to collect flowers, covering his chest and chin. Unwillingly, she leaves him and runs toward town to find help. She calls her mother from the nearest house.

Ironically, Grandpa's death, which should have helped the Pennoyers heal the fabric of their frayed family, only makes Jenny feel more alone and isolated. She hates the euphemisms they use to talk about him. She despises their lies. In a review in *Horn Book*, reviewer Mary M. Burns writes, "The denouement is tragic, not simply because the old man dies but because Jenny cannot reconcile her family's post-mortem commentaries with their actions toward the man who had once lived with them."[5]

After the Rain

The spine, or premise, of *After the Rain* can be found in a poem Mazer wrote in 1982 about the life and death of Michael Fox, her own father:

> I would like to write a poem
> For my father.
> This is the way it would start:
> For my father who died, etcetera.
>
> I would like to write a story
> About my father.
> This is the way it would start:
> This story is about my father
> Who lived an ordinary life.
>
> On the shelf I keep his glasses.
> Books held to his nose he read, he read.
> "I'm reading *War and Peace*," he said.
> "It's the fourth time."
>
> He was a milkman, a breadman—
> "I'm a route man," he said.
> World War Two, he worked in Alco—
> Fat times, $125 a week.
> "One-hundred twenty-five dollars," he said,
> "Let me see that check again."
>
> He died choking for air
> Strangled in a hospital bed—

Asbestosis.
Shipyard workers get it,
So do their families
Sniffing the dust in their clothes.

Hey, he was a route man
How come he died like that?

On the feeder, a cardinal, orange bill dipped in snow.
"Look at that bird," he said
As if he saw more than a blood-colored blur,
"Look at that bird, beautiful winter bird."

Once he pushed a broom
In a little tin-roofed factory,
Unpacked crates of asbestos.
"Only a couple weeks," he said,
"Two, maybe three weeks."

He died choking for air.
First of course he slowly got weaker—
One day he fell down in the street.
His sister had chemotherapy and died anyway.
"I hope my hair doesn't fall out," he said.

He died choking for air.
"Get the ticket," he said, "I'm taking the ship."
Months later I saw him—
(It was a dream of course)
I on a balcony, he below.
"Excuse me, Dad" (I was polite)
"Don't want to hurt your feelings,
"But you're supposed to be dead."

In *Summer Girls, Love Boys* (1982, 241-43)

After the Rain is the story Mazer wrote for her father. Even though the premise of the novel lived with her for many years, it took a long time to write this book about the relationship of an old, dying man with a young girl. That which made *After the Rain* a difficult book for Mazer to write also helps make it an outstanding book, a Newbery Honor Book. *After the Rain*, perhaps Mazer's most critically acclaimed novel, is her most sensitive work. One reviewer called it "a stunning portrait of two human beings."[6] There are marked similarities between it and *A Figure of Speech*. In fact, when Mazer told her agent she wanted to write a story about an old man who is dying and his relationship with his granddaughter, her agent said, "You've already written that book." So, Mazer put the idea away and seemingly forgot it.

In some ways her agent was correct—the spines of the two novels are similar. However, in more important ways her agent was wrong— each book is unique. *After the Rain* is a much better book—a more mature work of a gifted writer. It is a beautiful, heartfelt story that is more about relationship-building than about death. If *A Figure of Speech* is a handbook for how to tear families apart, then *After the Rain* is a primer for how to bring families together again. It is a book about learning how to love and how to care—Izzy has never been good at showing his love and so his granddaughter Rachel does it for both of them. By doing so she teaches Izzy and his estranged son and grandson about love and about life.

Izzy Shapiro is one of Mazer's most irascible, but somehow lovable, characters. Much like Mazer's own father, Izzy is very private and self-contained. He is old-fashioned, does not show his emotions often, and is proud of the work he has accomplished with his hands. Although he loves his family in his own way, he shows his love through criticism and rebuffs. Consequently, he is estranged from both his son Leonard and his grandson Jeremy. Rachel, who visits her grandfather with her parents each Sunday, resents these visits and feels smothered and embarrassed by her parents. They are old, as old as her friend Helena's grandparents. Rachel is the doted upon, much loved, unexpected youngest child of parents whose two sons are twenty years older than their sister. Rachel writes to her older brother Jeremy that she wishes their parents weren't so old.

Unlike the Pennoyers, the Coopers are a healthy family. Perhaps Izzy's own family was less so. His relationship with Leonard, his actor son, and Jeremy, his grandson and Rachel's brother, are fractured, but Rachel recognizes that her mother cares about Grandpa Izzy. She tells Rachel:

> "Grandpa was brought up differently . . . He wasn't born in this country. He doesn't understand about people like Jeremy and my brother Lenny. Grandpa was brought up that you should get a trade and stick with it, you should get married and stay married, that you should take a job,

work hard, and keep that job. He doesn't understand about
things like finding yourself, or being an actor, or trying out
new ideas." (28)

Mazer could be describing Michael Fox, her father, in this
passage. Or, she could be writing about one of her own grandfathers.

In *After the Rain* Mazer writes about more than the life and death
of her father, she writes about her entire family history. In Izzy live
her ancestors: the Gorelicks, her mother's parents, who came from
Poland, and the Foxes, her father's parents, who emigrated to London
and then the United States from the Ukraine. *After the Rain* is, in
many important ways, a compilation of all the stories she heard as a
child. Her paternal and maternal grandparents' families were troubled
and difficult—their world and lives had made them so. This novel is
the culmination of what Mazer enjoys writing about most—"the bonds
between people, the ways they're made and held and broken and
mended."[7]

Mazer laughs that in her youth she resented all her mother's
many stories—she always wanted her to get to the point. She thought
of her tales as lies rather than as stories. Today, she appreciates the
modified oral tradition in which she grew up—a tradition that has
given her a family history. *After the Rain*, of all her books, is the best
and most vivid example of Mazer's storytelling ability.

Izzy is also one of Mazer's most interesting, intriguing, and
honest adult characters. As a *Horn Book* reviewer concludes, his
"harsh, rough personality [is] so realistic and recognizable that we feel
we have known him and can understand the sorrow that overcomes
Rachel [after his death]."[8] Izzy is shy and reticent, much like Mazer's
father. He is not a good conversationalist. However, he, like Michael
Fox, gets along well with people outside of his family, particularly
women. Michael, Mazer reports, was a handsome man who, as a
breadman and a milkman, always got along with the women on his
route. In the novel, when Izzy falls in the street, much as Mazer's
father did as he became weakened by asbestosis, he is helped by Alice
Farnum. Alice is an attractive woman, and when Rachel goes to help
Izzy home she is surprised to find him flirting with Alice. Later in the
story Alice comes to check on Izzy, and Rachel notices that he enjoys
her visit and flirts with her again. "How easily Izzy is talking to Alice!
And he's telling her things he's never told Rachel" (145). This makes
Izzy real to the reader and more than an elderly grandfather to

Rachel—she begins to see him through the eyes of others. Like
Mazer's grandfather Aaron Garlen, Izzy is proud of his work as a
laborer—he believes that every man should have a trade, work with
his hands.

Mazer says of this story that she wrote it through faith. At the
beginning she had faith that the world of the story would begin to
appear. And it did. This book, like all of Mazer's novels, went through
several drafts. The last year she worked on the book, her computer was
having what she called "a nervous breakdown." She'd write a chapter
and come back the next morning and find it garbled or gone. For
several days things would be fine, and then suddenly she would lose
large sections or chapters would be mangled beyond recognition.
People told her computers didn't do things like that—it was her fault.
At first she believed them, but it kept happening, even as she was
trying to have the computer fixed. Finally, after trying many things
and failing, the computer expert who was fixing her machine threw up
his hands and said, "You have a ghost in the machine."[9] Mazer liked
that image, finding it appropriately literary. Given the book she was
writing, perhaps the ghost in the computer was more than a literary
allusion.

After the Rain is much more than a book about death; it is more
than a book about family unity and conflict. Although it is not
autobiographical, it may be the book that most allows us to enter the
author's heart.

The Cooper family is not perfect, but like all fully functioning
families, the Coopers work at living and loving. Every Sunday the
family goes to visit Shirley's father Izzy. Rachel dreads these days.
Izzy, like the men in Mazer's family, has strong opinions about
everything, but he is not much good at small talk. Once a week Rachel
telephones her grandfather, but neither has much to say to the other.

Shirley is worried about her father's health. He has trouble
breathing, he sweats a lot, and his complexion is gray. Rachel goes
with her mother when they learn Izzy's diagnosis: asbestosis. The
doctor has lied to Izzy—told him he has a clean bill of health. He tells
Rachel the truth—her grandfather will become weaker and weaker.

One afternoon when Rachel is home alone, she gets a phone call
from Alice Farnum about her grandfather falling on the street. When
she can't reach either of her parents, she goes to help Izzy get home.
He doesn't want her help, but she insists that if she doesn't walk him

home her mother will kill her. For the first time Rachel has the last word with Izzy. She begins to telephone Izzy to check up on him and unlike before, Izzy is really talking to her. Initially he is angry, defending himself, telling her he doesn't need or want her help, but soon Rachel realizes that even though he is complaining, they are having a real conversation. For the first time Rachel is feeling responsible for someone other than herself. She decides to begin walking each day with Izzy. "It's surprising she should make such a decision," suggests Cynthia Samuels, *Washington Post Book World* reviewer, "but once the reader accepts her choice and begins to join her on her daily visits with the crotchety old man, the story becomes both moving and wise."[10] At first Izzy acts as if he's being bullied, and Rachel thinks she would not walk with him if he weren't sick and having so much trouble breathing. As time goes on, Rachel enjoys their walks and conversations more and more, and Izzy seems to be waiting for her—anticipating with pleasure her arrival. One day when she goes out with her friend Helena, Izzy tells her he stayed in all day waiting for her. Rachel feels guilty and angry. She thinks of him as a tyrant, but her love is growing. Love, Mazer makes clear, comes from needing someone and being needed:

> What was it he said to her? "Do you think I have nothing else to do but wait for you?" And what about her? What about her life? Yes, yes, a voice jeers in her head, that's the way, you selfish, cold heart, compare yourself to an old, dying man. And then, coolly, the voice reminds her that while she did, indeed, go to work, before that she had plenty of time to drive around with her friends, have fun, and kiss Lewis in the park.
>
> She goes to Izzy's house the next afternoon, straight from school. (115-116)

"What distinguishes this book, making it linger in the heart, are the realistic portrayals of the tensions, guilt, and sudden, painfully moving moments involved in Rachel's and Izzy's situation."[11]

Slowly, he begins to open up to her, clamming up when she hits on a topic like Uncle Leonard. Izzy is also becoming weaker—some days he is unable to walk. One day Rachel and Izzy visit Grandma Eva's grave in the Jewish cemetery. It is that day that Rachel learns of Izzy's work as a stonemason and the pride he takes in it. Rachel is surprised when she hears herself ask Izzy, "Are you afraid of dying?" (138). He tells her, "Why be afraid of that? . . . You're born, you live, you die" (140). She wonders if he knows he's dying.

We learn through Rachel's journal entries about her daily walks with Izzy, his struggles, his failures, and her feelings. Through her reports of conversations with Izzy we learn about her strong, beautiful, little grandmother Eva who died the week after their fiftieth wedding anniversary, before Rachel was born. Izzy and Rachel's commitment to each other—their love—is growing.

Izzy is so proud of his work as a stonemason that a short time prior to his final hospitalization and death he takes Rachel on a bus trip to show her some of the bridges he has constructed. He tells her that on one, which they are unable to find while they are together, he put his initials and hand print. She goes searching for the bridge after Izzy's death, and it is this simple act which helps Izzy live on in Rachel. (A bridge, of course, is what Rachel is searching for both literally and figuratively.) When she finds the bridge with what Izzy called, "Five fingers and my initials, I.S." (245), she understands the importance of Izzy's mark and her discovery:

> They are here now, she thinks, and they will still be here years from now, when she, herself, is old. And then, though today the whole sky is covered by gray clouds, for a moment she feels the sun on her head, as warm as a living hand. (248)

When it's Helena's birthday they decide to have her party at Izzy's. He gets into the spirit of the party, dances with the young people, and tries to lift Helena to show how strong he still is. He collapses from the effort. A few days later he seems better again, telling Rachel he has seen Eva—not dreamed about her, seen her. That day they take a long walk, and Izzy seems appreciative of everything. They go for ice cream, and he seems like a young man to Rachel. But suddenly, he stops, nearly falling, and says, "I can't" (184). That day Rachel, Shirley, and Manny take Izzy to the hospital—he will never come home. Rachel decides to stay with him in the hospital and not go to school. At first he is ornery and feisty, but as time goes on he becomes weaker and weaker. The doctors keep lying to Izzy, telling him he will get better—he will go home. They say that they don't want him to lose hope, but Rachel is sure he knows he is dying. He goes through a period when he is very angry—he's in pain. However, when Alice comes to visit he makes himself welcoming to her. He sleeps more and more each day. He goes from not wanting anyone near him to not wanting anyone to leave him. He dies uttering the same words as Mazer's father:

> "I don't have my ticket," Izzy says. She turns. He is sleeping. His voice is low but clear. "Can I see the captain?" Then, a moment later, "Take another boat!" (221)

The family is close during the days following Izzy's death. Leonard cables and telephones from London. Many stories are shared. All of them are coming to terms with their love and dislike of Izzy. As one reviewer writes:

> This is a story all the more moving because Mazer preserves Grandpa's dignity as a character, so that both during his life and after his death, as Rachel adjust to loss, her grandfather is consistently taciturn and graceless—and the book speaks convincingly to the power of family love that is strong enough to accept this.[12]

He was who he was. They are able to live with that and share their pain and grief.

When She Was Good

When She Was Good, published in 1997, is Mazer's most powerful, mature, and darkest novel. According to critic Liz Rosenberg, "It is too dark, too complex, too brutal, too subtle, too brave and elegantly written."[13] Unlike all of her other novels, this one did not start out to be a young adult book. Mazer began working on it more than a decade earlier. It was always on her mind. She would be driving or walking, would see something, and would come home and write another bit. This went on for years—the book never left her. Initially, it was an adult novel about three women who came together through a series of unusual circumstances and found love in unique ways.

Mazer worked on the book on and off during this ten-year period. Each time she would get about two-thirds of the book written and then would come to a halt. She could not finish the novel, and she could not rid herself of it. Finally, a few years ago she decided that the only way to get the story out of her head was to "murder it." Harry convinced her there were too many good things in it to throw it away. So, she began anew. She wrote it every possible way—"first person, third person, shifting viewpoints . . ." When she was nearing the point beyond which she could not write, she happened to go to a Christmas party in New York City. She describes the party as the kind she truly hates: crowded, hot, and smoky. "The din was incredible." She decided to leave and was looking for Harry to tell him she was going home. At just that moment, she overheard a conversation about "real tough young adult stuff." At least, this is what she thinks she heard. She has no idea who the speakers were or if she really heard those words, but suddenly something clicked. Her adult novel needed to become a real tough young adult book. She could take Em Thurkill's story and make a book out of it. She had already written Em's horrifying childhood. This is something Mazer often does—not because she expects to use it in the book, but so she will come to know her protagonist. In the case of this novel, she crafted the stories of Em's childhood so that she would understand why Em was such an immature adult.

In a white heat Mazer began to race through the stored pages on her computer. She took everything she had written about Em and lined it up in a big file. When she was done she thought, "What am I going to do with this?" She had enough to begin, but she had to find Em's adolescent voice. Em could not be an immature adolescent—"the whole voice had to shift." Some of the book, such as the part in which Em and Pamela leave home, Mazer wrote during this period. However, it was not until she wrote the novel's first line—"I didn't believe Pamela would ever die" (3)—that she found Em's voice. And, according to critics, she captures her voice "beautifully: her fear as well as her desperation for normalcy and happiness as she struggles to survive on her own are both heart-wrenching and uplifting."[14]

The first line of the novel not only gives Mazer the voice she needs, it prepares her readers for a chilling tale of madness and abuse. The second line is no less powerful. "She was too big, too mad, too furious for anything so shabby and easy as death." This beginning will be remembered as one of the great opening lines of adolescent literature—ranked along with the first lines of Robert Cormier's *The Chocolate War* ("They murdered him.") and Lois Duncan's *Killing Mr. Griffin* ("It was a wild, windy, southwestern spring when the idea of killing Mr. Griffin occurred to them."). It is a first line that captures our attention and requires us to devour the book in one sitting. Frederick Busch, author of *Girls*, writes in a prepublication review of *When She Was Good*, " I read [the] devastating novel in one sitting, unable to stop. It is as powerful as a body blow, and it aches with the sorrowful effect of too many blows to the body and soul of a child."[15]

Mazer says that after she wrote the first line of the novel, she saw the form the book could take—"I saw the whole, complete thing." Mazer worked on the young adult book for about a year. During that time she was very excited. She says, "I had the feeling that it was the best thing I'd ever written." Reviews of the book and readers' reactions prove that she was correct. This is her best book—in this book she achieves excellence. Critic Dina Sherman calls the book "a stunning piece of fiction for readers mature enough to understand all its psychological complexities."[16] In its "Best Books" selection summary, *School Library Journal* calls the novel "a taut, introspective narrative."[17] Liz Rosenberg, in a *New York Times Book Review* feature article says that "it is written with a stinging clarity and conviction."[18]

Like a first novel, *When She Was Good* lived within Mazer for many years. Although it is a culmination of the promise of greatness and talent we have seen in Mazer since *A Figure of Speech* (1974), it is also a significant deviation from her previous work. It may well mark the beginning of a new period of literary maturity for this crafter of intriguing stories and composer of "brilliantly modulated language."[19]

In it, Mazer uses techniques she has perfected in many of her previous novels and short stories. The first sentence is the spine of her story. We know from the flashback approach she uses in the first few pages that Pamela is dead. Her descriptions are as vivid and simple as in earlier books. She artfully uses the rhythm of three: "Mr. Penniman has eyes like the eyes of certain dogs, either very nice dogs or scary dogs, I can't decide which" (7). The dialogue is natural and through it we come to know her characters. The book is a brilliant, first-person narrative told by Em. Like many of the other characters in Mazer's books, Em keeps a journal. Through the journal we learn not only about her today, but about her past and how her life has changed.

In *When She Was Good*, however, Mazer does much more. The book begins in the present—a terrifying present. Em is alone; Pamela has died. She is afraid of being alone—doesn't know how she will get beyond the funeral. However, she is more afraid that Pamela is not really dead—that she will break out of the coffin she is buying for her:

> My head heats up in two paths of fire. Suddenly I understand that Pamela is going to be put in a box, and it will make her furious. She will rise up, she will burst out, she will curse me and take me by the throat and pull me into the box with her. My heart stabs at my ribs. I know this can't be true, but what if it is? "I want the box locked," I say. (15-16)

The two sisters had been on their own for some time. Her mother died four years ago—Em recalls many things about her mother: her illness and her sweetness. She worries that her mother might not forgive her for Pamela's death. She remembers her mother calling to the two of them as they left the trailer on their way to school each morning—putting Pamela in Em's care.

Although we never know for sure what is wrong with Pamela, we know that she is disturbed. We know that she cannot control either her emotions or her actions. We know that Mrs. Thurkill, before she dies, and Em thereafter, feel a responsibility not only for caring for Pamela, but for controlling her. In this first chapter, in a section of the book called ironically "Earthly Comforts," we begin to understand that Em, even before her mother's unexpected death, has been alone with and responsible for Pamela. Simple sentences, straight-forward dialogue, carefully chosen words are an important element of this very tight novel. This is the kind of language, the carefully wrought dialogue, that has marked Mazer's work since her early short story collection *Dear Bill, Remember Me?* (1976).

The language of the novel is different, too. It is tougher, meaner, more tautly written. It is poetry rather than prose. Mazer "poetically evokes a poignant, honest image of rebirth and self-reliance."[20] She uses language in most of her novels sparingly—carefully selecting just the right word. However, in *When She Was Good* the language sings.

Late in the novel, for example, Em thinks about her problems and her fears:

> I discover that worry is no color, not even gray. And no shape, although it feels long and thin, like a cylinder rolled so tight you can never unloosen it. I discover that worry sits on your shoulders like something metallic and inanimate, a dead weight, but also breathing and alive, waiting to sink its metal claws into you. (194)

When She Was Good is also much darker and more mature than any of Mazer's previous works. It "often sounds like nonfiction—sort of a Very Young Liar's Club—not too good to be true, but too bad to be false."[21] There is so little hope. Everything potentially positive is turned into something horrifying. When Em writes in her journal, Pamela tears it up and flushes it down the toilet. Much later Pamela catches Em writing a few words on the back of a paper bag. Em tries to hide them, but Pamela is outraged, and she beats Em—sending her to bed with ice pressed against her swollen face.

Pamela is Mazer's most difficult and intense character. She is the true opposite of the kind, loving, diminutive Em who finds pleasure in simple things—in walks and in sunsets. Pamela is cruel, doing things just to anger those who care for her. She is terrifying. Em never knows what mood she will be in, nor does she know how long her current mood will last. Her gross weight makes her violence ominous.

Pamela is also Mazer's most eccentric character. Pamela's fourth-grade teacher, the only one who could tolerate her, once wrote to her mother, "she sometimes makes me think of a planet rocketing along in a parallel universe" (66). In one sad, humorous scene, Em attempts to tell the boy-minister who comes to the cemetery to do the funeral about her sister's "character." He wants to know what she was like so that he can comfort Em. The only things she can think of to say are: "She was Pamela." "My sister." "We lived together." "She liked to sit." "She liked to watch TV. She followed all the shows." (37-39) Between his questions and her brief declarative statements, Em remembers the real Pamela. She can't tell him these things:

> Pamela's smile was real, made your heart jump when it appeared. The surprise of it. The relief. The second surprise of her teeth: small, like baby teeth, and white,

very white. It must have been in her genes. She never
brushed, she said it was a waste of time, but her teeth
were beautiful . . .

They must have had to stuff her into the coffin. This
last year she had become fatter than ever. Fat was on her
everywhere, pillows of fat on her arms and neck and
around her waist and ankles. She liked being fat. She liked
having massive arms and legs. She liked eating and sitting
and doing nothing. She had one chair in front of the TV
and one by the window, where she could watch the
parking lot . . .

Her favorite chair was the one in front of the TV, and
when she left it to sit in the other chair, she had a special
joke. "Em!" she'd call. "I'm taking my exercise now." (37-
38)

In spite of the horror of this scene, it is very funny. We chuckle at
the minister's attempt to say something nice about Pamela.

In this novel, as in some of her earlier novels, the act of cutting
hair symbolizes coming of age. However, in this novel it is much more
dramatic. One day, soon after Em and Pamela have moved into their
own apartment—Em has a job and they have food in their
refrigerator—Em invites her mother's distant cousin to visit them.
Mary Uth is an old lady, and Em does not tell Pamela of the
impending visit. After Pamela recovers from the surprise, she screams
and becomes abusive. *"Old bitch frucking bag of bones did you ever
come to see our mother do you even care she died get that disgusting
ugly face away from me or I'll puke on your head"* (29). Pamela grabs
Mary by the shoulders and throws her out the door, slamming it
behind her. Shortly thereafter she begins dragging Em around the
apartment by her braids. Em cuts her hair, little by little, so that
Pamela will not notice, afraid of retribution if Pamela discovers that
Em has kept her from this painful game by cutting her hair.

The novel is divided into three sections: Earthly Comforts, In the
Reign of Pamela, and The Doubled Moon. This is the first time Mazer
has used this approach, and it serves this story well. The first section
tells us, in flashbacks remembered while Em is picking out a coffin
and again at the funeral, of Pamela's death, their mother, and their life
alone together. Em also returns home to the trailer they had shared
with their mother and father. She learns how difficult it is to go home
when she finds herself sneered at while sitting, inconspicuously, in the

town library—a place that had previously been a sanctuary for her. Throughout this section of the novel, Pamela is dead, but she keeps talking to Em who can't get her out of her mind.

The second section of the novel is a flashback to their years in the trailer and their early years together in the city. We learn that their father became abusive when he was drunk. Em was thirteen when her mother became ill with the flu and Em found her dead under the heaped blankets. Immediately after the funeral, their father took all their mother's belongings to the dump. Em was able to salvage only one old, green sweater with cat buttons. This scene, reminiscent of the scene in which Mrs. Pennoyer packs up Grandpa Carl's possessions to give them to the Salvation Army in *A Figure of Speech*, provides evidence of Mazer's growth as a writer. In *When She Was Good* the actions of Mr. Thurkill are characteristic of the egocentricity of the man. They help define who he is, and are important, cruel evidence of the horrifying aloneness Em is experiencing. Her only happy memories are of her mother and all she has left is a moth-eaten sweater. In the earlier novel the scene seems contrived to move the plot, but in *When She Was Good* the scene is simple, yet critically important to our understanding of Em's plight.

It is from this moment that their father withdraws from the girls' lives. Although his presence had never been a positive one, at least he was there, and when he was sober he could help control Pamela. From the moment he packs up his dead wife's belongings, he begins to fade, literally and figuratively, from their lives. Pamela quits school and at her father's insistence gets one job after another. She becomes increasingly abusive. Em is lonesome, and, in one of the novels most poignant scenes, she begins to let boys, first one and then others, have their way with her. "As long as they were nice, I let them do what they wanted, and sometimes it was so sweet—their eager voices, their hands, the way they said "Please" and "Oh, Em" (86-87). She is just fourteen.

Although things are certainly not good at home, they get worse when their father marries Sally. She changes everything in the trailer and even has their mother's car painted. She insists the girls get jobs and pay room and board for their keep. One day Pamela finds money Sally had hidden, and the girls agree to use it to run away from home. Em is not yet fifteen.

When they get to the city they lie about their ages and rent an apartment. In the beginning it is a friendly, relatively happy time, but then the money runs out, Pamela stops paying the rent, and they are evicted from the apartment—all their belongings put out on the curb. At first the girls sleep in the bus station. They go to a shelter. During the day when they have to leave the shelter, they go to the library or the ladies lounge of a large department store. The social worker convinces Pamela to go to a psychologist and helps Em get a job at a food counter in a variety store. Things appear to be looking up when the social worker helps them find an apartment.

Pamela begins to knit dolls—Monica dolls—and optimism fades:

> She talked about it as if it were alive. She perched her on the back of the couch and warned me not to pick her up. "She doesn't like anyone but me to touch her." She said that the Monica—and, later on, the first Mortie—was there to watch me. (121)

Em loses her job and then a series of other jobs. Each day when she comes home the first things she sees are the dolls. Pamela is becoming increasingly violent and abusive. Em is almost sixteen. After losing a job because Pamela keeps calling her at work, Em buys a bus ticket to Burlington, Vermont. Realizing her need to escape and the potential danger of her life with Pamela, Em stays in Burlington for a week. She is angry and afraid, but she also feels guilty about leaving her sister. One day Em calls Pamela, and when Pamela agrees not to hit her anymore—even though she tells Em it was her fault— Em allows herself to be persuaded to go home, thinking that her sister has missed her. She, too, is lonely and needs Pamela.

At the start of the third section of the novel, there are more Morties and Monicas who watch Em every minute of every day. When she can stand it no longer, Em knocks the six Morties and six Monicas to the floor from their perch on the back of the couch. In spite of the beating she endures as a consequence, Em remains hopeful—tending her bruises in silence. She still hangs on to the belief that happiness will be given to her, if she is good.

The section shifts to shortly after Pamela's death, but thoughts of Pamela—the sound of her voice—still live with Em. "Her voice was in my head, in the air, in the room" (146). One day Em breaks the lock off Pamela's cupboard and finds all of the things she had "lost" over the years: garnet earrings that had been her mother's, the green sweater, a china dog . . .

In *When She Was Good* Mazer goes beyond the truism of the unity of family to begin an exploration of whether unity outside of family can repair a damaged person. The novel provides no answer, but leaves the reader to ask new questions. Will Em survive on her own? Will Em develop friendships? How will Em pick up the pieces of her life? Did her past damage her beyond repair, sentencing her to a grim future? Can an individual survive without the unity of family?

Em begins to search for a life outside of the family, but has no idea how to begin. She sees a woman coming through the front door of the apartment building and dreams of their becoming friends, but she doesn't know how to talk to her. Em tries to convince the maintenance man to allow her to plant a flower garden, but even this fails. We begin to despair with Em—there seems to be no hope:

> A familiar feeling overtakes me: a heaviness in the legs, a
> thickness like dust in my head. It won't happen. Nothing
> will change. I can't have what I want. I groveled in front of
> this man for nothing. I'm so stupid. Just what Pamela
> always said. (156)

But we are beginning to understand that Em will not be defeated. Her natural optimism will allow her to survive. She goes out and looks for another job.

One day Em learns the name of the dark-haired woman, Louise D'Angelo, by retrieving a discarded envelope from a wastebasket in the mailroom of the apartment house. She has still not found her voice—she has not spoken to her. She fantasizes about a friendship with the woman, even going up to her apartment and looking at her front door. She does not knock.

Em is alone and lonely—she has never been alone before. Even at her worst, Pamela was company for her sister. Em begins to plant a flower garden, even though she has been told she cannot, turning the earth with a cheap trowel. It is hard work, but she is happy. She finally finds Louise coming out of a bakery carrying an armload of long, fresh loaves. Em realizes that this is where Louise works. When Louise discovers her outside the bakery door she accuses Em of following her.

We are afraid for Em, not sure how long she can survive without work and without friends. One day she sees Louise and asks her to

take a splinter out of her finger. Louise is puzzled and refuses. Em
feels bad. "My face aches as if Pamela were squeezing it. That's it, I
think. That's the end. I feel so bad" (190). One rainy day while on her
way to find work, she runs into a homeless woman wheeling a cart.
The woman tells her that she used to be like her. She is a beggar. Em,
who is still not seventeen, thinks, "She is to me as I am to Louise:
supplicant, beggar, someone desperately trying to convince someone
else of her worth" (193).

Em is beginning to feel worthless. She has no money, worries all
the time, feels alone and unwanted, and can't find a job. However, she
does not give up. In spite of her optimism, nothing seems to go her
way. But just as hope seems to be gone, Em runs into Warren Weir, a
man she calls "St. Toothbrush," and realizes she has a friend. That day
she finally is rid of Pamela. "She is quiet now. She is gone. She has
left. Standing in the doorway, I understand this at last" (208). The
next day she finds a job and is paid in advance.

When she waits for Louise one day on the landing, the older
woman tells her she does not want to be her friend. She says she is not
a nice person, even her own daughter doesn't like her or want to see
her. Em says she still wants to be Louise's friend, but Louise walks
past her. One rainy day she sees Louise on the street—she sees a look
in her eye that she interprets as "leave me alone." She walks on, alone,
through the rain. When she is almost run over by a taxi, Louise comes
up to her. "You jerk!" Louise shouts at the retreating cab. "He would
have rolled right over you," she says. Louise holds her green umbrella
over Em. "He drenched you" (226). Em finally has a friend.

In the next to the last chapter we finally learn how Pamela died.
Em is, for the first time, able to remember the horror of her sister's
death. Pamela's voice is no longer constantly in her head, screaming
at her. The apartment is quiet. And, now, finally, Em is able to begin
to deal with the guilt she feels for not being sorry that Pamela is dead.
"Sorry, and not sorry. Sorry she's dead. Not sorry she's not here"
(231). The book ends with a final, optimistic chapter. Em is
remembering—not the horrifying memories or the awful days with
Pamela, but the comforting memories of picking elderberries with her
mother. The book ends with hope—hope that comes with harvesting
fruit and working together to turn it into sweet jam. Em's final
thoughts are optimistic ones: "And, oh, it was so good" (234). We

don't know if she will be able to say this about her life, but we do know that she will be able to go on.

Little Domestic Situations

Without a doubt, Mazer's novels, as she says, are "little domestic situations." They take place inside families. Family to her is the central unit of life providing our ultimate sense of unity—our place in the world. Without family we are diminished, and, indeed, Mazer is not sure there is hope for the individual when family is gone. Mazer recognizes and chronicles the many problems of family life and relationships—the biggest of which cause total erosion of its unity.

At Harry's urging, she gave Em more hope at the end of *When She Was Good*, but it is not clear whether she really believes Em can survive without family. Mazer and her readers may discover in future works whether her protagonists can lead productive lives without being part of a family unit. Mazer will explore this issue in a second novel about an older Sarabeth Silver who loses her mother in the first chapter and must survive on her own. She may also eventually complete her adult novel about Em—a novel she actually began to write many years ago, long before Em came to life in *When She Was Good*. It is likely that the reason she was not able to write this adult novel is that she had not convinced herself that Em could survive on her own, without family. Perhaps, after writing about Sarabeth alone, she will be able to return to this long-abandoned work.

When Mazer calls her work "little domestic situations" she is underestimating her enormous talent. Yes, her works—almost all of them—take place in families. To date, this setting has been essential to her fiction because it is in this ultimate unity of the family that Mazer believes we find our most extreme conflicts—what she calls the unity of opposites. *When She Was Good*, her most mature work, seems to suggest that she may be able to move away from this setting, this unity of family, and explore relationships outside of it.

Centering her fiction in families does not diminish her great talent, nor does it suggest that her work is not varied, that all of her fiction is the same. She sometimes worries about this, but she is wrong—Mazer's range is immense. She has published novels in many genres: realistic fiction, romance, science fiction, suspense, and mystery. Probably by the time this book is released, Mazer's readers will be devouring her next novel, a work of historical fiction, titled in manuscript *Goodnight, Maman*. Her short stories are even more varied—that is probably why she has found writing her short story books most rewarding. Few writers have the ability to craft so many different types of fiction.

The techniques she employs within her novels and short stories are also diverse. She is equally comfortable writing in first, second, or third person. Her dialogue is accurate and revealing, including letters, journals, diaries, essays, and audiotapes to help us get inside the heads of her characters. She successfully shifts the voice in her novels—often more than once, and writes equally well from the male or female perspective—an element that has improved as her writing has grown in maturity. Her characters are well rounded and even her minor characters are developed—more so in her later work. Because of this we can empathize even with those characters who should not be likeable. Her work is carefully crafted and tightly written. Rarely do we find an unnecessary sentence or word. Her descriptions place us with her characters and we walk with them through life. Perhaps Mazer has not yet found a story that "will make it all clear," but she has helped her readers come closer to an understanding of themselves and their ultimate reality. Mazer's talents as a writer are enormous, and, best of all, she continues to grow.

Notes

1. Norma Fox Mazer, "Why I Write. . . . Why I Write What I Write," *The ALAN Review* (Spring 1987): 50.
2. Karel Rose, "The Young Learn About the Old: Aging in Children's Literature," *The Lion and the Unicorn* (Winter 1979-80): 64-75.
3. Hildegarde Gray, review of *A Figure of Speech*, *Best Sellers* (November 16, 1973): 382.
4. Jill Paton Walsh, review of *A Figure of Speech*, *The New York Times Book Review* (March 17, 1974): 8.
5. Mary M. Burns, review of *A Figure of Speech*, *Horn Book* (April 1, 1974): 152-153.
6. Mary Lystad, review of *After the Rain*, *Twentieth-Century Children's Writers* (1989): 652.

7. Norma Fox Mazer, "Why I Write. . . ," *Indirections* (September 3, 1990): 9.
8. *Horn Book* Review of *After the Rain*, in *Contemporary Authors*. Vol. 32. James G. Lesniak, ed. (Gale Research Company, 1991): 291.
9. Mazer, "Why I Write. . . ," 8-9.
10. Cynthia Samuels, review of *After the Rain*, *Washington Post Book World* (May 10, 1987): 19.
11. Review of *After the Rain*, *Kirkus Reviews* (May 1, 1987): 723.
12. Review of *After the Rain*, *Voices of Youth Advocates* (June 1987): 80.
13. Liz Rosenberg, "Problem Child," *The New York Times Book Review* (November 16, 1997): 32.
14. Dina Sherman, review of *When She Was Good*, *School Library Journal* (September 1997): 221.
15. Frederick Busch, "Advance Praise for *When She Was Good*," in Norma Fox Mazer, *When She Was Good*, Advance Reader's Edition (Scholastic Press, 1997). Book jacket.
16. Sherman, review, 221.
17. "Best Books," *School Library Journal* (December 1997): 26.
18. Rosenberg, "Problem Child," 32.
19. Busch, "Advance Praise for *When She Was Good*." Book jacket.
20. Review of *When She Was Good*, *Publishers Weekly* (July 21, 1997): 202.
21. Rosenberg, "Problem Child," 32.

Bibliography

Primary Sources

Books

Mazer, Norma Fox. *A, My Name Is Ami*. New York: Scholastic Inc., 1986.

——. *After the Rain*. New York: William Morrow, 1987.

——. *B, My Name Is Bunny*. New York: Scholastic Inc., 1987.

——. *Babyface*. New York: William Morrow, 1990. New York: Avon.

Mazer, Norma Fox and Harry Mazer. *Bright Days, Stupid Nights*. New York: Bantam, 1992.

Mazer, Norma Fox. *C, My Name Is Cal*. New York: Scholastic Inc., 1990.

——. *D, My Name Is Danita*. New York: Scholastic Inc., 1991.

——. *Dear Bill, Remember Me? And Other Stories*. New York: Delacorte Press, 1976. New York: Dell Publishing.

——. *Downtown*. New York: Avon, 1984.

——. *E, My Name Is Emily*. New York: Scholastic Inc., 1991.

——. *A Figure of Speech*. New York: Delacorte Press, 1973. New York: Dell Publishing.

——. *Goodnight, Maman*. New York: Harcourt Brace, 1999.

Mazer, Norma Fox and Harry Mazer. *Heartbeat*. New York: Bantam, 1989.

Mazer, Norma Fox. *I, Trissy*. New York: Dell Publishing, 1971.

——. *Missing Pieces.* New York: William Morrow, 1995. New York: Avon.

——. *Mrs. Fish, Ape, and Me, the Dump Queen.* New York: E. P. Dutton, 1980. New York: Avon. Reissued as *Crazy Fish.* New York: William Morrow, 1998. New York: Avon, 1998.

——. *Out of Control.* New York: Avon, 1993.

——. *Saturday, the Twelfth of October.* New York: Delacorte Press, 1975. New York: Dell Publishing.

——. *Silver.* William Morrow, 1988. New York: Avon.

Mazer, Norma Fox and Harry Mazer. *The Solid Gold Kid.* New York: Delacorte Press, 1977. New York: Bantam Doubleday Dell.

Mazer, Norma Fox. *Someone to Love.* New York: Delacorte Press, 1983. New York: Dell Publishing.

——. *Summer Girls, Love Boys and Other Short Stories.* New York: Delacorte Press, 1982.

——. *Supergirl* (a novel based on a screenplay by David Odell). New York: Warner Books, Inc., 1984.

——. *Taking Terri Mueller.* New York: Avon, 1981.

——. *Three Sisters.* New York: Scholastic Inc., 1986.

——. *Up in Seth's Room.* New York: Delacorte Press, 1979. New York: Dell Publishing.

Mazer, Norma Fox and Marjorie Lewis, eds. *Waltzing on Water: Poetry by Women.* Dell Publishing, 1989.

Mazer, Norma Fox. *When She Was Good.* New York: Scholastic Press, 1997.

——. *When We First Met.* New York: Scholastic Inc., 1982.

Short Stories

Mazer, Norma Fox. "Cutthroat." In *Ultimate Sports: Short Stories by Outstanding Writers for Young Adults,* ed. Donald Gallo. New York: Delacorte Press, 1995. New York: Bantam Doubleday Dell.

——. "The House on Buffalo Street." In *Night Terrors,* ed. Lois Duncan. New York: Simon & Schuster, 1997.

——. "I, Hungry Hannah Cassandra Glen . . ." In *Sixteen: Short Stories by Outstanding Young Adult Writers,* ed. Donald Gallo. New York: Delacorte Press, 1986. New York: Dell Publishing.

——. "In the Blink of an Eye." In *When I Was Your Age: Original Stories About Growing Up,* Vol. 2, ed. Amy Ehrlich. Cambridge, MA: Candlewick Press, 1999.

——. "Meeting the Mugger." In *Places I Never Meant to Be,* ed. Judy Blume. New York: Simon & Schuster, 1999.

——. "Tuesday of the Other June." In *Short Takes: A Short Story Collection for Young Readers,* ed. Elizabeth Segel. New York: Lothrop, Lee & Shepard, 1986.

——. "What Happened in the Cemetery." In *Visions: Nineteen Short Stories by Outstanding Writers for Young Adults,* ed. Donald Gallo. New York: Delacorte Press, 1987.

Articles and Chapters

Mazer, Norma Fox. "Bread, Books, and Passion." In *Signal* (1988-1989): 1-3.

——. "Breathing Life into a Story." In *The ALAN Review* (September 1995): 13-15.

——. "Censorship and the Writer." In *Alki: The Washington Library Association Journal* (July 1986): 72-74.

——. "Comics, Cokes, & Censorship." In *Top of the News* (January 1976): 167-170.

——. "Growing Up with Stories." In *Top of the News* (Winter 1985): 157-167.

——. "I Love It! It's Your Best Book!" In *English Journal* (February 1986): 26-29.

——. "The Ice-Cream Syndrome (aka Promoting Good Reading Habits)." In *Authors' Insights: Turning Teenagers into Readers & Writers,* ed. Donald Gallo. Portsmouth, NH: Boynton Cook, 1991.

——. "Letters to Me." In *The ALAN Review* (Spring 1990): 8-11.

——. "Norma Fox Mazer." In *Something About the Author Autobiography Series,* Vol. 1., ed. Adele Sarkissian. Gale Research Company, 1986.

——. "Thirty Seconds, Eight Drafts, Three Years—and Then a Book." In *The Writer* (December 1993): 19-20.

——. "Three Teachers." In *The ALAN Review* (Fall 1988): 52.

——. "*Up in Seth's Room*: Some Thoughts." In *The ALAN Review* (Fall 1980): 1.

——. "What's the Big Idea, Anyway?" In *Hot Flashes: Women Writers on the Change of Life,* ed. Lynne Taetsch. Boston, MA: Faber and Faber, 1995.

——. "When You Write for Young Adults." In *The Writer* (February 1986): 15-17.

——. "Why I Write. . . ." In *Indirections* (September 3, 1990): 6-22.

——. "Why I Write. . . . Why I Write What I Write." In *The ALAN Review* (Spring 1987): 49-50.

——. "'Write as Though You Were Talking to Me': Kids, Letters, and Writing." In *English Journal* (March 1990): 63-64.

——. "Write Me Soon." In *The Address Book of Children's Authors and Illustrators,* ed. R. Howard Blount. New York: T. S. Denison & Co., 1994.

——. "Words from Norma Fox Mazer." In *Writing!* (March 1987): 18.

——. "Words on a Ketchup Bottle." In *The ALAN Review* (Fall 1991): 2-5.

Secondary Sources

Books and Parts of Books

Bowden, Jane A., ed. *Contemporary Authors* (vols. 69–72). Detroit, MI: Gale Research, 1978.

Commire, Anne, ed. *Something About the Author Autobiography Series* (vol. 2). Detroit, MI: Gale Research, 1981.

Helbig, Alethea K. and Agnes Regan Perkins, eds. *Dictionary of American Children's Fiction, 1960-1984.* New York: Greenwood Press, 1986.

Holtz, Sally Holmes. *Presenting Norma Fox Mazer.* Boston, MA: Twayne Publishers, 1987.

Metzger, Linda, ed. *Contemporary Authors* (New Revision Series, vol. 2). Detroit, MI: Gale Research, 1984.

Olendorf, Donna, ed. *Something About the Author Autobiography Series* (vol. 67). Detroit, MI: Gale Research, 1992.

Stine, Jane C., ed. *Contemporary Literary Criticism* (vol. 26). Detroit, MI: Gale Research, 1983.

Articles and Speeches

Mazer, Harry. Speech, ALAN Workshop, St. Louis, MO. Unpublished (November 1988).
McLaughlin, Frank. "A Conversation with Norma Fox Mazer." In *Writing!* (March 1985): 18-21.
Rose, Karel. "The Young Learn About the Old: Aging in Children's Literature." In *The Lion and the Unicorn* (Winter 1979-80): 64-75.
Rosenberg, Liz. "Problem Child." In *The New York Times Book Review* (November 16, 1997): 32.

Reviews

Abrahamson, Dick. Review of *Taking Terri Mueller.* In *The ALAN Review* (Spring 1982): 15.
Burns, Mary M. Review of *A Figure of Speech.* In *Horn Book* (April 1, 1974): 152-53.
———. Review of *Downtown.* In *Horn Book* (January/February 1985): 61.
Busch, Frederick. "Advance Praise for *When She Was Good.*" In *When She Was Good,* Advance Reader's Edition (Scholastic Press, 1997).
Campbell, Patty. Review of *Up in Seth's Room.* In *Wilson Library Bulletin* (October 1979): 123, 139.
Chelton, Mary K. Review of *Someone to Love.* In *Voice of Youth Advocates* (October 1983): 206.
Codell, Cindy Darling. Review of *Missing Pieces.* In *School Library Journal* (April 1995): 154.
Cooper, Ilene. Review of *Taking Terri Mueller.* In *ALA Booklist* (December 1, 1981): 500.
———. Review of *Out of Control.* In *The New York Times Book Review* (May 16, 1993): 29.
Eaglen, Audrey B. Review of *Someone to Love.* In *School Library Journal* (Spring 1983): 137.
Ebbatson, Trish. Review of *Heartbeat.* In *School Library Journal* (June 1989): 124.
Flowers, Ann A. Review of *Dear Bill, Remember Me?* In *Horn Book* (February 1977): 58-59.

Forman, Jack. Review of *Saturday, the Twelfth of October*. In *School Library Journal* (November 1975): 93.

——. Review of *The Solid Gold Kid*. In *School Library Journal* (September 1977): 148.

Fritz, Jean. Review of *Up in Seth's Room*. In *The New York Times Book Review* (January 20, 1980): 30.

Gray, Hildegarde. Review of *A Figure of Speech*. In *Best Sellers* (November 16, 1973): 382.

Horn Book Review of *After the Rain*. In *Contemporary Authors*. Vol. 32, ed. James G. Lesniak. Detroit, MI: Gale Research Company (1991): 291.

Lystad, Mary. Review of *After the Rain*. In *Twentieth-Century Children's Writers*. Chicago, IL: St. James Press (1989): 652.

——. Review of *Mrs. Fish, Ape, and Me, the Dump Queen*. In *Twentieth-Century Children's Writers*. Chicago, IL: St. James Press (1989): 652.

Noah, Carolyn. Review of *Out of Control*. In *School Library Journal* (March 1993): 222.

Pollack, Pamela D. Review of *Dear Bill, Remember Me?* In *School Library Journal* (October 1976): 191.

Ritter, Karen. Review of *Taking Terri Mueller*. In *School Library Journal* (December 1981): 67.

Samuels, Cynthia. Review of *After the Rain*. In *Washington Post Book World* (May 10, 1987): 19.

Sherman, Dina. Review of *When She Was Good*. In *School Library Journal* (September 1997): 221.

Stevenson, Deborah. Review of *Out of Control*. In *Bulletin of the Center for Children's Books* (April 1993): 259.

Sutherland, Zena. Review of *Babyface*. In *Bulletin of the Center for Children's Books* (November 1990): 65.

——. Review of *Bright Days, Stupid Nights*. In *Bulletin of the Center for Children's Books* (May 1992): 242.

——. Review of *Heartbeat*. In *Bulletin of the Center for Children's Books* (July/August 1989): 124.

Walsh, Jill Paton. Review of *A Figure of Speech*. In *The New York Times Book Review* (March 17, 1974): 8.

Wersba, Barbara. Review of *Saturday, the Twelfth of October*. In *The New York Times Book Review* (October 19, 1975): 12.

Wooldridge, C. Nordhielm. Review of *Summer Girls, Love Boys*. In *School Library Journal* (November 1982): 102.

———. Review of *When We First Met.* In *School Library Journal* (February 1983): 91.

Zvirin, Stephanie. Review of *Bright Days, Stupid Nights.* In *ALA Booklist* (June 15, 1992): 1826.

———. Review of Summer Girls, Love Boys. In ALA Booklist (October 1, 1982): 198-199.

After the Rain

In *Kirkus Reviews* (May 1, 1987): 723.
In *Voice of Youth Advocates* (June 1987): 80.

C, My Name Is Cal

In *Kirkus Reviews* (December 1, 1990): 1676.

Dear Bill, Remember Me?

In *Kirkus Reviews* (October 1, 1976): 1101-1102.

Taking Terri Mueller

In *Contemporary Authors,* Vol. 32. Ed. James G. Lesniak. Detroit, MI: Gale Research Company (1991): 290.
In *Kliatt Young Adult Paperback Book Guide* (January 1982): 13.

Three Sisters

In *Bulletin of the Center for Children's Books* (March 1986): 133.

Up in Seth's Room

In *ALA Booklist* (November 1, 1979): 440.
In *Kirkus Reviews* (December 1979): 1380.

When She Was Good

In *Publishers Weekly* (July 21, 1997): 202.

Index

About the Author

Arthea J. S. (Charlie) Reed, *professor emeritus* at the University of North Carolina at Asheville (UNCA), is currently Director of Agency Development and Long Term Care Specialist at the Asheville Agency of Northwestern Mutual Life/Baird Securities. From 1989 to 1995 she was chairperson of the Department of Education at UNCA. A professor of education from 1978 to 1996, she has taught courses in adolescent literature, English methods, foundations of education, and research. She has written fifteen books including *Presenting Harry Mazer, Reaching Adolescents: The Young Adult Book and the School, Comics to Classics: A Guide to Books for Teens and Preteens, In the Classroom: An Introduction to Education,* and *A Guide to Observation and Participation in the Classroom.* She is coeditor of the Penguin USA teachers' guide series and is author of many guides on classic books. She has written CD-ROM scripts for several of the guides.

Charlie Reed was the 1995-1996 president of ALAN, the Assembly on Literature for Adolescents of the National Council of Teachers of English. She was editor of *The ALAN Review* from 1984 to 1990. Her faculty colleagues at UNCA honored her by naming her the 1985-1986 Feldman Professor for teaching, scholarship, and service. She has taught at every level, from elementary through graduate school, in four states.

Dr. Reed lives on a mountaintop near Asheville, North Carolina, with her niece Stephanie, her husband, two dogs, and a cat. She is active in volunteer work and serves on the United Way cabinet and the board of Carolina Day School, both in Asheville. For relaxation, she likes to play golf, walk on the beach at her second home in Hilton Head, South Carolina, and hike on the trails near her mountain home.